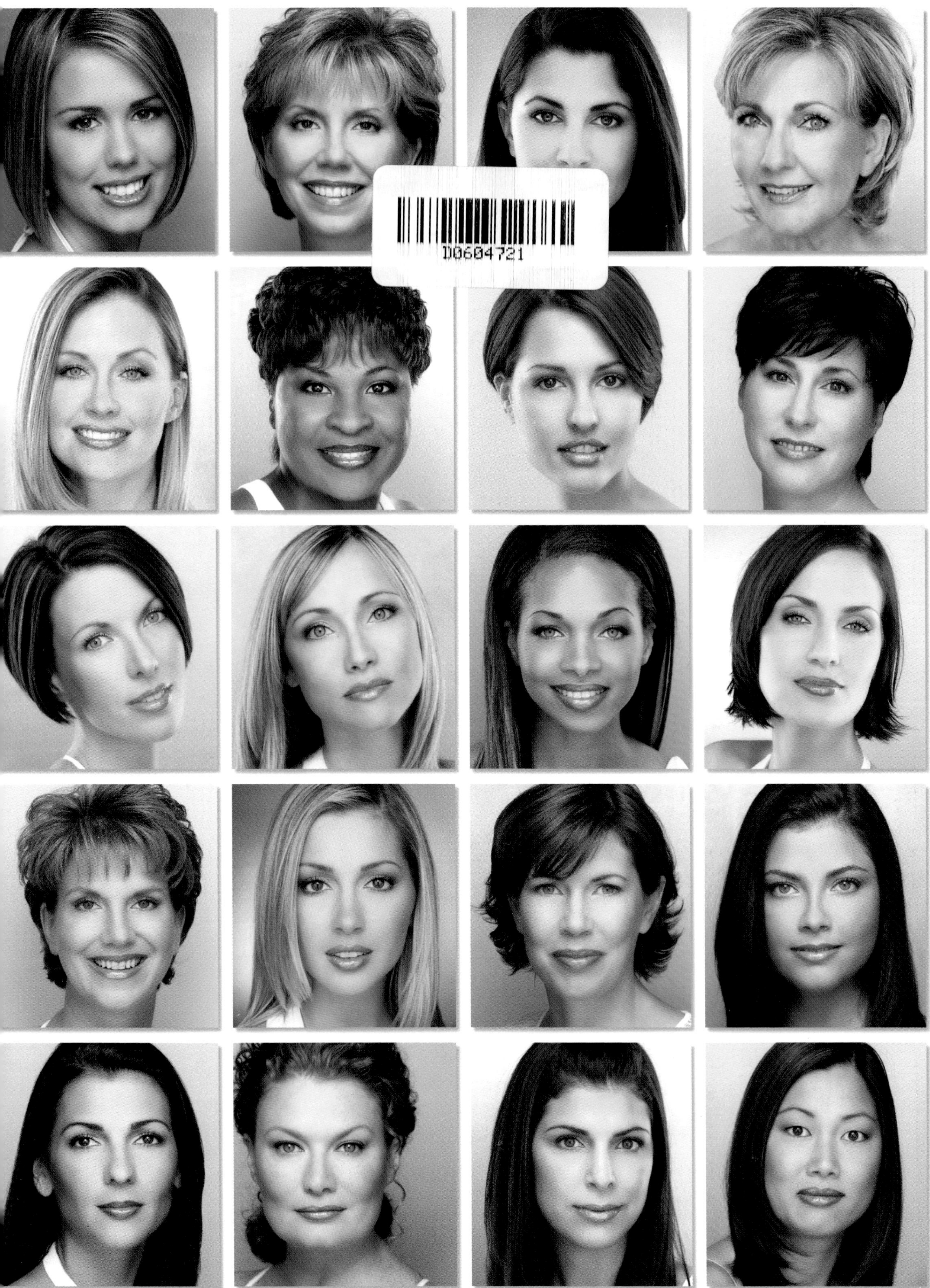
D0604721

beauté made simple

a make-up guide by robert jones
written with patricia young

ISBN 0-9717241-0-5

Hair & make-up: Robert Jones accompanied by Susie Jasper

Representation: Seaminx Artist Management www.seaminx.com

Producer: Tiffany Mullen

Fashion photography: Jeff Stephens

Fashion stylists: Barri Martin and Deborah Points, Amy Simmonds (assistant stylist)

Still-life photography: Fernando Ceja

Still-life stylist: Linda Jantzen

Behind the scenes photography: Cindy James

Design and Art Direction: The Glassmoyer Group, Inc. New York City

www.beautémadesimple.com

This book is dedicated to three very special people who have passed through my life, each of which I believe are now watching from above as guardian angels: my grandmother, Carolyn Walker Scoville (left), who was one of my first ideals of beauty; Bernardo Aldrete, no one ever believed in me more; and finally Diane Payne (right), a true inspiration.

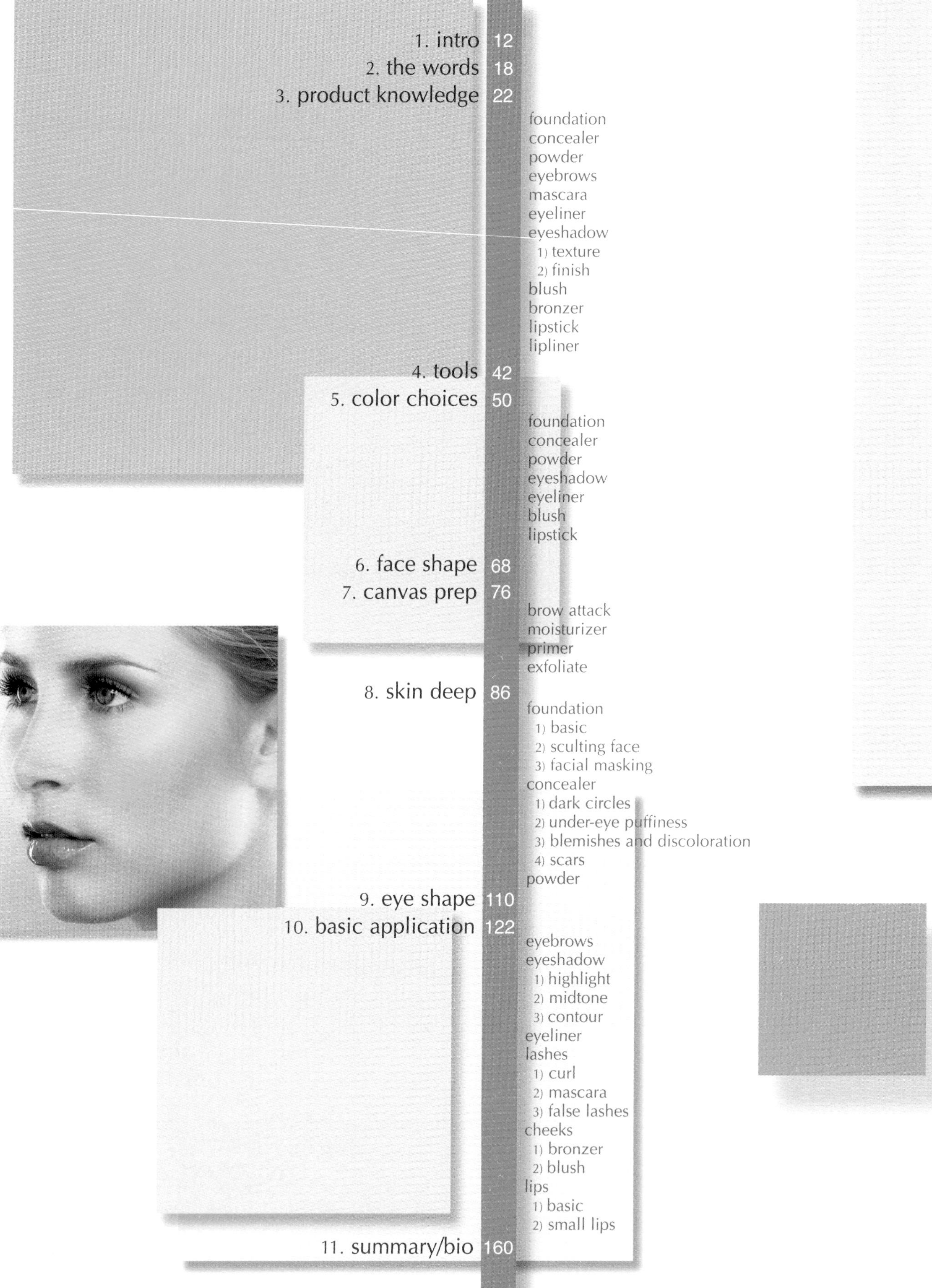

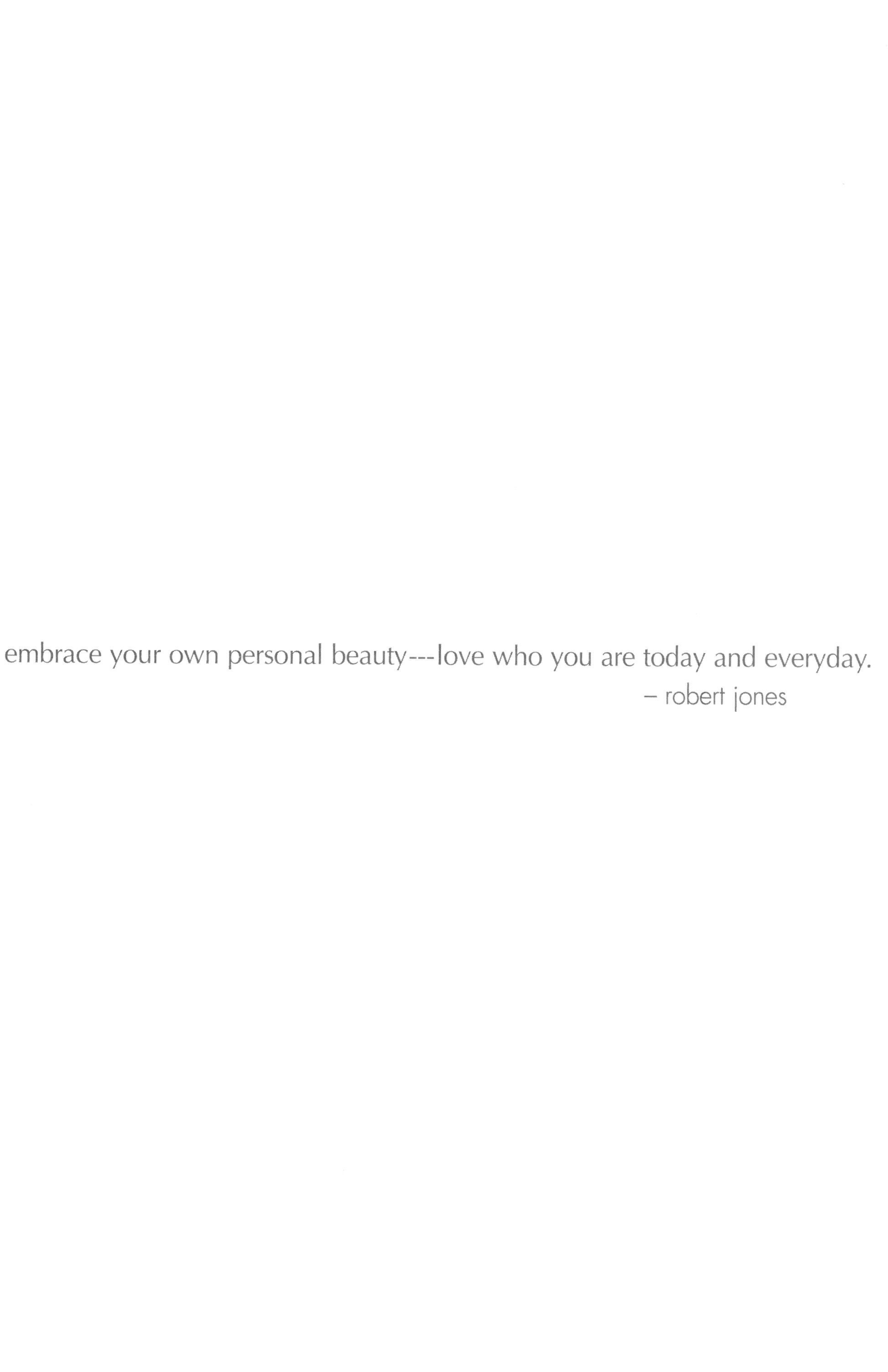

embrace your own personal beauty---love who you are today and everyday.

– robert jones

This book is all about you---who you are, who you want to be and who you can be. I truly feel that every woman is beautiful. It is just a matter of recognizing your beauty and making it your focus.

I have long been convinced that beauty is not just about possessing a perfectly symmetrical face. Obviously it's marvelous to be blessed with exceptional features, but not all of the women I've made up in my many years as a professional makeup artist were flawless. Some of the most beautiful women I have ever seen or worked with are beautiful because of who they are and what comes from within. Beauty comes from the expression and character in your face---not just it's symmetry. It doesn't matter if you are short or tall, heavy or thin, or if your features aren't those of a fashion model or famous actress. Your beauty comes from self-awareness, self-confidence and your own magnetic personality. Actually, I feel that self-confidence is the most important element of true beauty.

My goal in writing this book is to help you bring out that beauty from within by increasing your self-confidence about your outward appearance. I want to demystify the art of makeup and help you understand how to use it as a tool to better appreciate who you are. Some women think makeup is far too difficult to master, but it's simple when you break it down. It's merely a matter of using the right products, good tools and the correct techniques.

"First and most importantly every woman needs to remember she is beautiful."

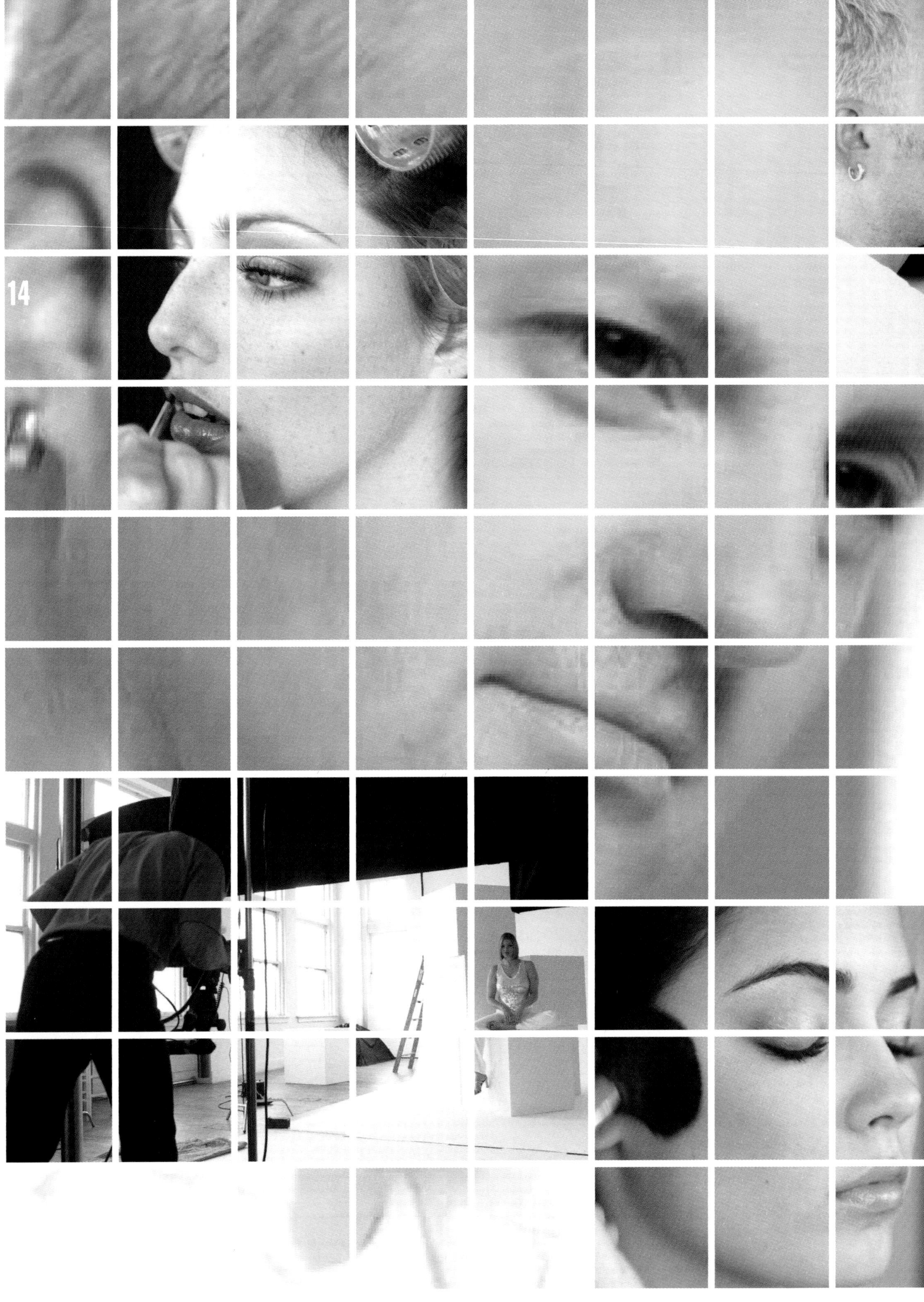

First and most importantly let me say that every woman needs to remember she is beautiful. By identifying your most striking features and accentuating them, we can make you look and feel more beautiful. Certainly one of the reasons I love being a makeup artist is the joy it gives me when I see how my work can change the way you feel about yourself. No matter what your age, if you are beautifully made up with bright eyes and a healthy glow, you will exude an aura of confidence that will draw people to you.

Modern makeup should be simple and natural so it's the face we notice not the makeup. I feel that cosmetics are to enhance the features God gave you, not to change them. I'm not suggesting natural makeup means walking around all day looking washed out. By simple and natural, I mean your makeup palette should be suited to your complexion and should change with each season to compliment the change in your skin's natural tone. Sometimes I'll notice a woman who obviously has made an effort with her makeup but has chosen a foundation color that's all wrong for her skintone, or she's wearing a lip color that's far too dark or vivid for her. The concept that "less is more" definitely holds true for makeup.

Makeup is meant to be beautiful, and beautiful makeup is all about the colors you use and where you place them---never about how much you put on. I also think that it is important to remember that the face is not flat. It's not one-dimensional therefore don't paint it that way. Makeup should be used to artfully sculpt and accentuate your best features---that is the very essence and purpose of wearing makeup.

Keep in mind that there are very few hard-and-fast rules in makeup and beauty. Beauty is in the eye of the beholder. And since beauty is subjective, everything discussed in this book reflects my own personal views. Each professional makeup artist has his or her own style, as do each of you. Mine has been described by many as the 'Glamorous-Girl-Next-Door'---I guess because I think all women should look beautiful but be approachable, and a little glamour never hurts. I want to help you discover your own personal style. Whatever the season or event, beautiful makeup will boost your self-confidence, which in turn will make you feel good about yourself, which will translate into true beauty. So read on---experiment with your makeup---have fun with it, and together we'll discover a more self-confident and beautiful you.

"Makeup is meant to be beautiful, and beautiful makeup is all about the colors you use and where you place them---never about how much you put on."

Now here are some of the key words I'll be using throughout my book followed by a brief explanation of each. I thought it would be helpful to define them so you would better understand what we are talking about.

matte
n satin
dewy
sheer eyeliner
earlescent
gloss
aque powder
w metallic
concealer

1. MATTE: (mat) is used to describe lipsticks, eye shadows, foundations, powders and blushes that have absolutely no shine and appear flat. Matte lipsticks tend to be drier, but they stay on much longer. Matte foundations are excellent on shiny and oily skins and are best for skins with imperfections. There are also matte products such as powders and cremes that will help fight oils during the day.

2. SHIMMER: (shim´ər) is the opposite of matte. It sparkles and shines because it contains tiny iridescent particles. Shimmery products usually have a combination of colors that create the sparkle. They look superb on dark skin tones.

3. SATIN: (sat′ ′n) refers to a formulation that's neither as flat as matte nor as shiny as shimmer. "A satin soft and silky finish" is an often-used description of foundations and liquid cosmetics that give a soft, smooth finish to the skin. Satin products have a sheen to them, but they're not shiny. Satin eye shadows are particularly good for older skins because they glide on smoothly and have a soft sheen to them.

4. PEARLESCENT: (pʉrl es′ent) products that are not as shiny as shimmer yet they have a definite glimmer. Pearl-tones liven up the skin and are in eye shadows, cheek colors and lipsticks. They look wonderful on Asian skins but appear too light on dark skins.

5. GLOSS: (glôs, gläs) is a super high-shine lipstick with short staying power.

6. IRIDESCENT: (ir′i des′ənt) is about maximum sparkle and super-shine. Iridescent is a fun, sexy look and works best on young skin because on more mature skin it can draw attention to the fine lines. The term is usually used in reference to eye shadows and lip glosses.

7. METALLIC: (me tal′ik) describes lipsticks, eye shadows and eye pencils that have a shiny, metal finish. It's a look that is fantastic on ebony or darker skins but too harsh for lighter or older skins.

8. FOUNDATION: (foun dā′shən) is a miracle product that evens out your complexion and covers all imperfections. Your foundation's tone depends entirely on your skin. If your skin is looking radiant and beautiful without help, then by all means skip the foundation and go to a light dusting of powder. However, if you do need foundation, it comes in a variety of texture finishes such as matte, satin and dewy. If you have oily or blemished skin, choose the matte. If your skin is normal or dry, you can chose from any of the finishes.

9. DEWY: (doo′ē) often refers to foundation finishes that create a fresh and glowing look with a slight sheen.

10. LUMINESCENCE: (loo′mə nes′əns) describes a foundation with light-reflecting qualities that creates a glowing, refined look. The light-reflecting properties contain specially shaped particles that bounce light away from surface lines and wrinkles to create a more youthful look.

11. SHEER: (shir) is a thinner and more transparent finish that gives the skin a lovely glow. It usually contains silicone that allows the makeup to glide on easily. The product clings less and covers more smoothly without being opaque. Sheer products seem to disappear into the skin, giving it a softer more natural appearance. Sheer foundation is fabulous for mature women since it helps older skin look brighter and less lined. And it's great for younger skin that just needs a little evening out.

12. OPAQUE: (ō pāk') is a finish that provides absolute coverage, allowing nothing to show through.

13. CONCEALER: (kən sel'ər) is a miracle product that hides everything your foundation didn't. It will make broken capillaries and under-eye circles, age spots and any skin discoloration disappear.

14. POWDER: (pou'd ər) is for setting foundation. It gives your face a smooth finish and keeps shine under control.

15. BLUSH: (blush) is for adding both a wonderfully warm glow and a gentle shaping to the face. It can brighten the dullest of skin. If your cheeks are naturally rosy you might skip the blush and leave the glow up to Mother Nature.

16. EYELINER: (i'lin'ər) for defining and "bringing out" the eyes, though it is not always necessary.

17. EYESHADOW: (i'shad'ō) is either applied lightly as a gentle color-wash or as a more dramatic layering of color and texture to enhance and add shape to the eyes.

18. MASCARA: (mas kar' ə) is to give you those full, long, thick and dark lashes you've always wanted. If I've just described your natural lashes, just using an eyelash curler may be all it takes to spotlight your baby blues, browns, grays, hazels or greens. If marooned on a desert island, mascara would be most women's number one choice for the makeup they'd most like to have marooned right along with them.

19. LIP COLOR: (lip kul' ər) is the quickest way to set the mood of your overall look. You can go all out and define your lips with color, or you can smear a clear gloss or healing lip balm for that pared-down, natural look.

20. TEXTURE: (teks'chər) is the finish a product gives you---the way it appears on your skin. For example, when referring to blush, it could be creamy, powdery or dewy. When referring to foundation, it could be dewy, creamy, sheer or satin. Lipstick could be glossy, matte or sheer. Texture is currently the industry's catchphrase for foundation. There are exceptions, of course, but generally speaking it's wise to always match your textures---powder on powder, crème on crème.

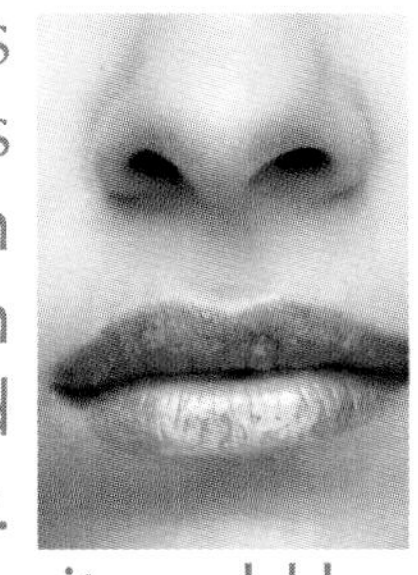

3 product knowledge

This chapter is to help you understand more about the products that are out there and how to use them. So many of them come in a variety of formulas and textures. This information will help you choose which product will work best for you and your application skill level.

foundation

is for most women their favorite product and their least favorite product. Most wear it and some of those who do hate wearing it. It's probably the one product that's the hardest to choose correctly.

When making your choice, there are two important considerations to bear in mind. The first is to match your skin tone and depth, so that your foundation looks natural. Secondly, it is also very important to match the needs of your skin type with the correct foundation formula. For example, using the wrong formula on oily skin can cause the oils to mix with the foundation, making it look patchy by shifting the color. It will also affect how long the foundation does or does not stay on.

Your foundation is your most important makeup investment, so if you were to ask me directly, I'd advise you to spend wisely. The important thing to remember is that the variance in the cost of cosmetics from one company to another is not only in the packaging but also in the ingredients used. The purer the ingredients, the more expensive a product will be. Products formulated with purer ingredients contain a higher quality of pigments. The cheaper product lines generally contain fewer and inferior pigments that won't wear as long. If you want to cut costs I'd advise you to do it on fun color products rather than on foundation or powder, which are the bases of everything and therefore the most important elements. If you want to treat yourself and splurge on something, by all means please make it your foundation.

Two very important characteristics of foundation that you need to think about are texture and formulation. The varying formulas and textures provide different sorts of coverage and finishes. The consistency---the texture and the way it actually goes onto the skin---is just as important as the product itself. Thanks to modern technology, we now have many advanced products to work with that when applied can appear almost invisible. The real goal for your foundation is for it to look as if you're not wearing any at all; you simply give the illusion of having healthy and beautiful skin.

foundation generally comes packaged in eight different forms:

STICK foundation is essentially a neatly packaged crème-foundation and concealer in one. Best for normal to dry skin, it is a good option for women who want more coverage. It offers ideal, maximum coverage for imperfections as well as covering ruddy and uneven skin tones. Stick foundation will give you quick coverage, but it can look a little heavy on clear skin where a lot of coverage is not needed.

LIQUID foundation is the most readily found and is suited to most---if not all---skin types. It is available from oil-free formulas all the way to moisturizing formulas and gives varying degrees of sheer-to-medium coverage depending on the brand and the formula. You can purchase liquid foundation in a bottle or a tube. When applied, it gives you more coverage than a tinted moisturizer but less than a crème foundation.

CRÈME foundation is smooth and milky and is specifically formulated for drier complexions. It gives the skin a natural finish while offering the highest coverage. I find it to be the most versatile because even though it tends to be of a thicker and heavier consistency it can be made sheerer simply by applying it with a damp sponge. Also, because of its great coverage, it can even be used as a concealer if you don't have severe under-eye circles. Crème foundation is great for dry skin; however, if you have dry flaky skin, beware, because it can look "cakey" and the result can be slightly dull and heavy-looking.

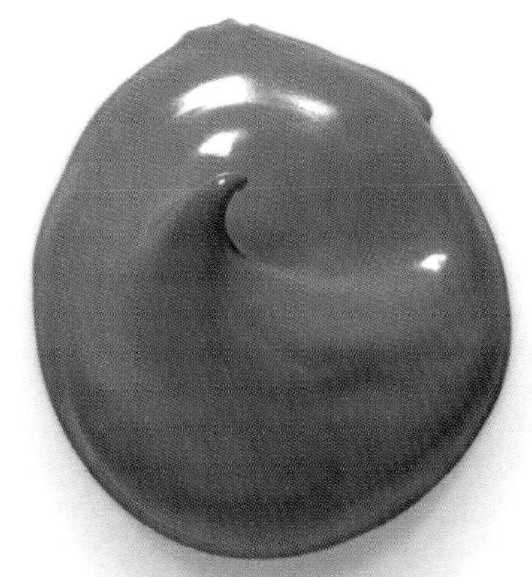

MOUSSE foundation is actually a crème foundation that has a whipped consistency. It generally comes in a jar rather than a compact, and it is usually lighter and sheerer than its compact counterpart. It evens out the skin tone without appearing heavy. I use mousse-textured formulas a lot because they seem to sink into the skin rather than sit on top of it. They give great coverage that appears very natural. They are fabulous on mature skin because they do not collect in fine lines like heavier crème formulas.

TINTED moisturizer is actually a moisturizer with a little color added. It's the sheerest of all the foundations, and it's perfect for use during the summer months when you feel like wearing next to nothing. It evens out the skin tone while providing minimal coverage.

CRÈME-to-POWDER foundation is quick and simple. It has a creamy texture that dries to a powder finish, so usually no additional dusting of powder is needed to set it. These formulas are kinder to oily skin than their crème counterparts because the powder helps cut down on excess shine.

POWDER COMPACT is dual-finish powder-foundation that gives a quick and convenient sheer-to-medium coverage. It is simply a pressed-powder that is formulated to be used wet or dry. Used dry, it goes on like a pressed-powder but gives you more coverage. I find that used dry it's perfect for young girls because it's low in oils and doesn't clog pores, therefore there's little risk of pimples appearing without warning. Used wet, it gives you more complete coverage, much like most other liquid and crème foundations. And it's great for touch-ups when you're on the go.

PIGMENTED MINERAL POWDER is simply a loose powder that adheres to the skin, providing medium to full coverage. In addition to giving you coverage it also contains vitamins and minerals to help treat the skin. It works much like a dual-finish powder foundation and is simple to apply, with a brush or a sponge.

concealer

comes in various formulations and textures. Different textures of concealers are used on different problem areas, so it's important to match the texture with the problem area. For example, a concealer used to cover under-eye areas should always be moist and creamy, whereas a concealer designed to cover breakouts or broken capillaries should be much drier in texture so it will adhere better and last longer.

SOLID CREAM STICK concealers give full coverage but are not always the easiest to blend. They are used primarily for hiding some of the more prominent blemishes and skin discoloration. They can also be used to minimize under-eye circles, but if you're going to use this texture make sure the consistency is creamy enough to blend well so as not to accentuate fine lines. Since the most delicate skin is under the eyes, using a hard-to-blend stick concealer can actually make the circles look far worse by drawing attention to them.

POT CONCEALER provides similar coverage to stick, but it is usually formulated with more moisturizing ingredients and is not quite as thick---much better for underneath the eyes. This is the concealer that's probably the most commonly used by professionals because of the great coverage it gives. Although usually creamy, it is also available in drier, oil-free formulas that are used to cover discoloration on the rest of the face.

TUBE CONCEALER generally has a creamier texture that's lighter and less likely to collect in fine lines, therefore making it great for mature skin. It provides terrific coverage and is useful because it can be further thinned by mixing it with foundation. It's perfect to use under the eyes because it's one of the easiest to blend.

WAND CONCEALERS offer the lightest texture and are excellent for evenly smoothing skin tones. If the proper shade is used, you may apply it without a foundation because it will blend easily into bare skin. Wand concealers provide a quicker, slightly denser coverage than liquid foundation, and they're absolutely fabulous for a fast repair. Some dry to a powder-finish that's great for covering facial blemishes because the powder clings, enabling it to be longer wearing.

PENCIL CONCEALERS effectively cover tiny imperfections such as broken capillaries, blemishes and other tiny flaws. You simply draw it on. With an exact color-match they can be pinpointed without blending. Pencil concealers are also terrific for fixing lip lines.

OIL-FREE COMPACT CONCEALER formulations are best used on the face to hide pimples and spots. They are usually of a longer-wearing, drier texture that won't irritate breakouts. Because of their wearability they are also effective for covering age-spots and hyper-pigmentation.

HIGHLIGHT REFLECTING products thankfully are now available. They help to hide flaws but don't actually cover. Instead they have light-reflecting properties that refract light to help minimize shadowed areas. In other words they highlight (bring out) recessed areas such as the dark shadows created by bags and wrinkles. You simply apply it to the shadowed area, and it brightens it, making it appear less distinct. You should apply them sparingly. Too often they are confused with concealers, which they most definitely are not!

powder

Powder is indispensable. It is absolutely not a step to skip. Makeup won't last the day without powder. You can even brush it over a clean, moisturized face for a fresh no-makeup look.

Most face powder is made from two bases---cornstarch and talcum. It basically comes in two forms, loose and pressed. Use a loose powder to set your makeup. It works the best and lasts the longest. Of course, if you travel, pressed powder is far more convenient to take along with you. Powder is an absolute must for oily skin. One thing I can't stress strongly enough is that the finer a powder is milled, the higher the quality, so the less likely it is to cake.

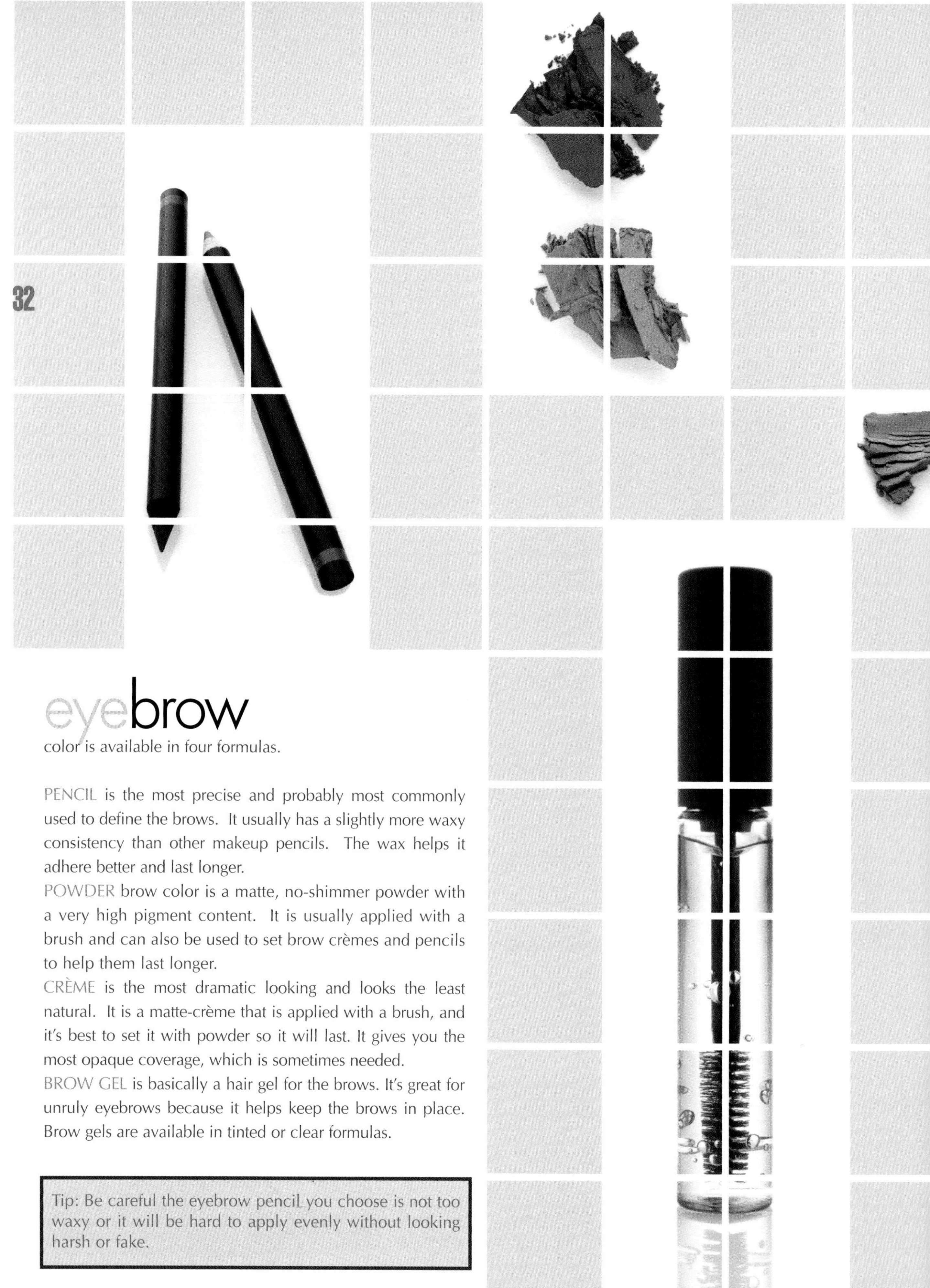

eyebrow

color is available in four formulas.

PENCIL is the most precise and probably most commonly used to define the brows. It usually has a slightly more waxy consistency than other makeup pencils. The wax helps it adhere better and last longer.

POWDER brow color is a matte, no-shimmer powder with a very high pigment content. It is usually applied with a brush and can also be used to set brow crèmes and pencils to help them last longer.

CRÈME is the most dramatic looking and looks the least natural. It is a matte-crème that is applied with a brush, and it's best to set it with powder so it will last. It gives you the most opaque coverage, which is sometimes needed.

BROW GEL is basically a hair gel for the brows. It's great for unruly eyebrows because it helps keep the brows in place. Brow gels are available in tinted or clear formulas.

Tip: Be careful the eyebrow pencil you choose is not too waxy or it will be hard to apply evenly without looking harsh or fake.

mascara

generally comes in three formulas.

THICKENING mascara coats each individual lash from root to tip with particles that add bulk to the lashes and help them to look thick and full.

LENGTHENING mascara contains plastic polymers that cling just to the tips of the lashes, making them appear longer.

DEFINING mascara coats each individual lash, keeping them separated and defined. Defining mascara usually appears the most natural.

Most mascara is also available in a waterproof formula. However, unless you're susceptible to pesky allergies that make your eyes water, I really don't recommend waterproof mascara because it's harder to remove and therefore can be damaging to delicate lashes.

Most women don't realize that the mascara wand is just as important to the finished result of your lashes as the mascara formula.

There are four basic brush shapes.

-- A crescent-shaped wand that helps curl the lashes up as you apply your mascara.

-- A fat, bristly wand that helps to thicken by coating each and every lash.

-- A wand that looks much like a screw, that either has very short bristles or none whatsoever. It allows you to define your lashes by painting each one right down to the root.

-- A double-tapered wand is a wand with smaller bristles at each end, tapering to fatter ones in the center. It works very nicely to define each thin, sparse lash while adding a little bulk.

It's always better to apply two thin coats of mascara rather than one thick, "clumpy" coat. I personally prefer thick, voluminous-looking lashes. I think they help define the eyes, and they look so much more glamorous than thin, spidery-looking lashes. Now with new technology, some formulas claim to lengthen and thicken at the same time.

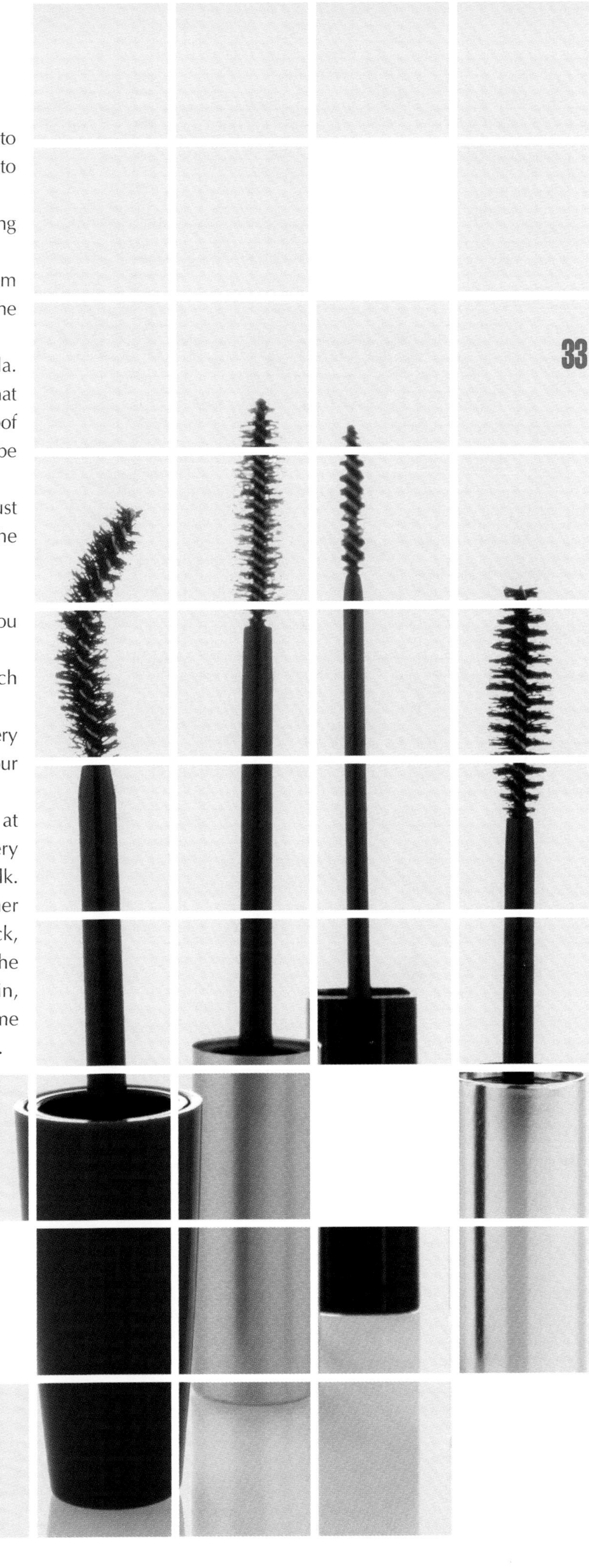

eyeliner

comes in four basic formulas.

LIQUID eyeliner is a colored liquid that dries to a matte finish. It is applied with a fine-tip brush. Liquid will stay the longest and look the most dramatic. There are also liquids available in felt-tip pens or with a pointed, sponge-tip applicator. Liquid is used in conjunction with strip false eyelashes because it successfully hides the band of the lash.

CAKE eyeliner is a pressed powder-like product that is applied with a damp brush. It will give you a similar effect to liquid eyeliner, but it's much easier to control.

CRÈME eyeliner is usually packaged in a pot and is applied using a damp brush. It will also give you a similar effect to liquid eyeliner. The fact that it dries much quicker makes it much easier to use without smearing it all over the place.

PENCIL is the most commonly used simply because it's the easiest to control. There are many pencil textures available. Some are drier and quite hard, and some are creamier and glide on quite effortlessly. In the past many women have felt the need to soften their hard, dry pencils using a lighter or a match. Thankfully, because of advanced technology, most pencils now contain silicone that enables them to glide on smoothly and makes them easy to smudge and blend.

Tip: Remember that sharpening your pencil often will make it easier to use.

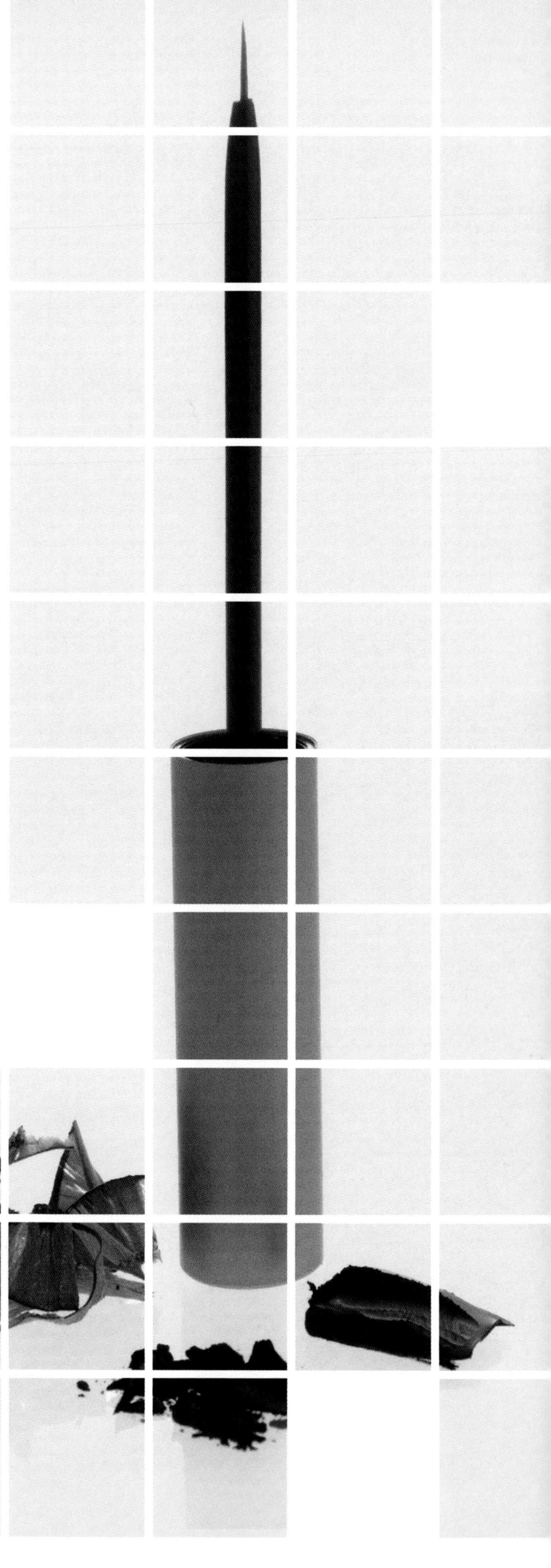

eyeshadow

comes in various textures and finishes.

TEXTURE:

POWDER SHADOWS come either loose or pressed. Both formulas vary from matte to shimmer and from iridescent to frosty. They are the most popular and the easiest to use because they blend so well. In most makeup lines, they offer the largest color choices in this texture.

CRÈMES are available in matte and shimmer. They are great used for a wash of color across the entire lid. Be careful because most crème shadows can crease. However, there are some crèmes that dry to a powder finish.

LIQUID usually comes in a shiny, metallic finish and it's actually the hardest to use. Since it doesn't blend easily you must be more precise, so it's best when applied with a brush. Liquid is usually used either as an eyeliner or applied close to the lashline for color intensity.

PENCIL shadows are useful for around the eye because they are sharpened to a point and can be applied with such precision. When you've finished, you can simply smudge the line with your finger, a sponge-tip applicator or a brush to create the effect you want.

Tip: For a more intense color, try using both powder and crème shadows together.

Tip: Remember that powder on top of crème will hinder blending, so always begin with the crème. It contradicts the rule of crème-on-crème, powder-on-powder---but it works.

Tip: You can also use your powder shadow as eyeliner. Simply apply it wet or dry using a brush.

Tip: Some powder shadows are harder pressed and more powdery, while others have a slight creamy texture.

all four types of shadows come in a variety of finishes.

MATTE is the best for creating a natural no-makeup look and is the most preferred for mid-tone defining because of its natural appearance. It usually contains a higher level of color pigment and works really well for reshaping and defining the eye.

SHIMMER is formulated by combining two or more shiny color particles to create more sparkle and shine than frost. Because of its high sheen quality, light-shimmer shadows work great for highlighting and bringing out the recessed areas of the eyelid. Also, the fact that it is sheerer than frost allows it to be quite effective on mature skin. Dark shimmer shadow colors work great for adding drama without being as harsh as deep-tone matte shadows.

FROST unlike shimmer is formulated from a single color of sparkle. It's usually much more opaque, and because the frost can sink into wrinkles it usually does not work as well on mature skin. Frosty shadows are most often found as light pastel shades.

OPALESCENT/ PEARLESCENT. As the word suggests an opalescent product simply provides an opal-like finish. Opalescent eye shadows are usually light in color-depth.

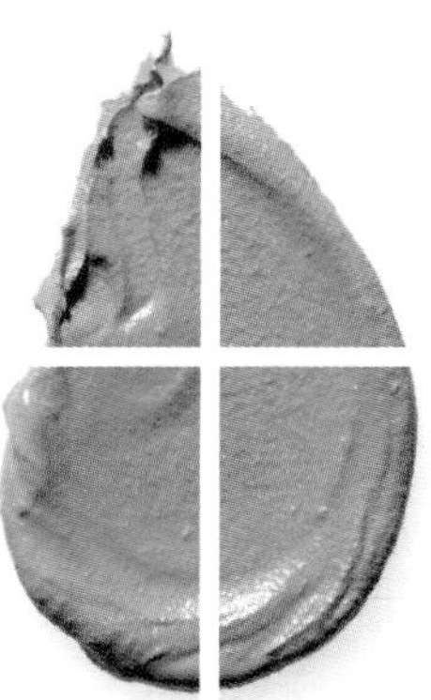

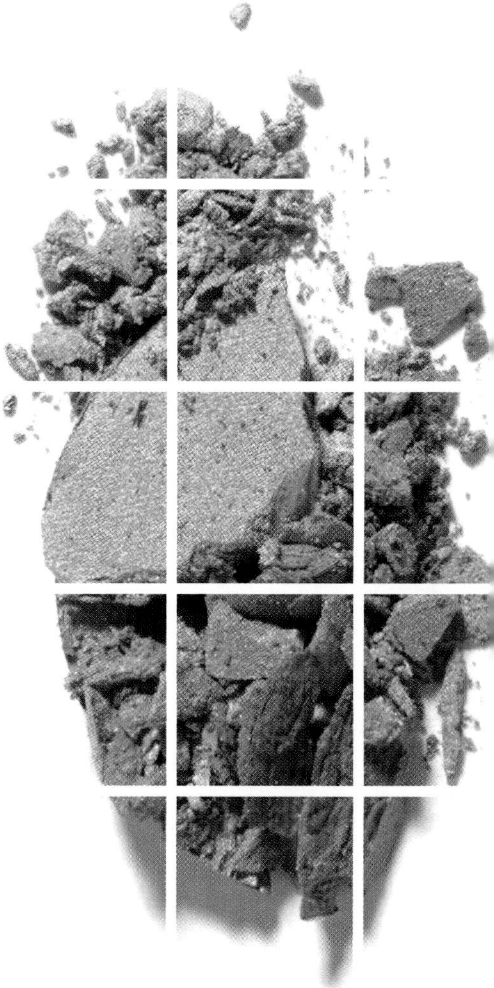

blush

usually comes in four different textures.

POWDER BLUSH is color pigment set in a powder base. Applied with a soft blush brush it gives a dusting of color that works well with all skin types. It's the most popular type of blush because it's the easiest to control and use---and it's usually available in the widest range of shades.

CRÈME BLUSH is color pigment set in a crème base. It has a fresh dewy finish that gives the face a luminous, natural glow. It is great on dry skin because it slides easily over the surface. It works best when applied before you powder because it will blend more easily. Unfortunately, if you have oily skin, crème blush is not your best choice because it won't wear well. And it doesn't work well on skin with large pores because it tends to accentuate them. It's great for those who don't need or want to wear foundation. Just apply it with your fingers or a sponge and work it into your skin.

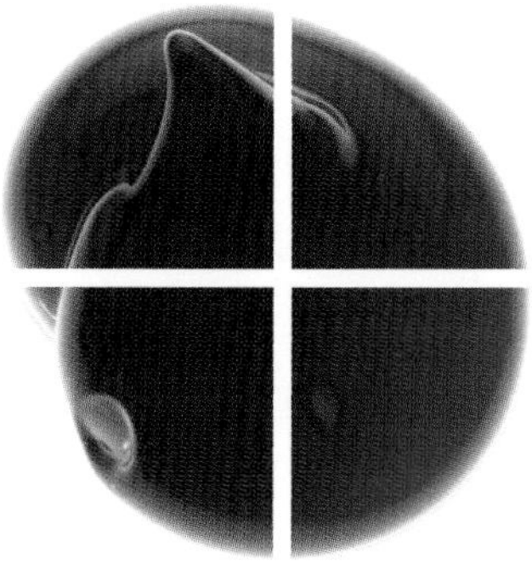

GEL BLUSH is basically made up of color pigments that are wrapped within silicone particles. It will smooth very nicely onto bare skin to create a pretty, sheer, translucent glow. It's not to say you can't use it with foundation; you can. Just make sure you apply it before you powder. It's long lasting, looks very natural, and it's easy to use. You can use your fingers or a sponge to apply it, then smooth it into the skin.

LIQUID BLUSH is actually a liquid that stains the skin. It's terrific for all skin types. It applies like the gel blush, but it's a little more difficult to work with as it must be blended quickly, because of its staining quality. It's waterproof so you can expect it to last all day. Just as with crème blush or gel blush, you can use either a sponge or your fingers to apply and blend it well into your skin.

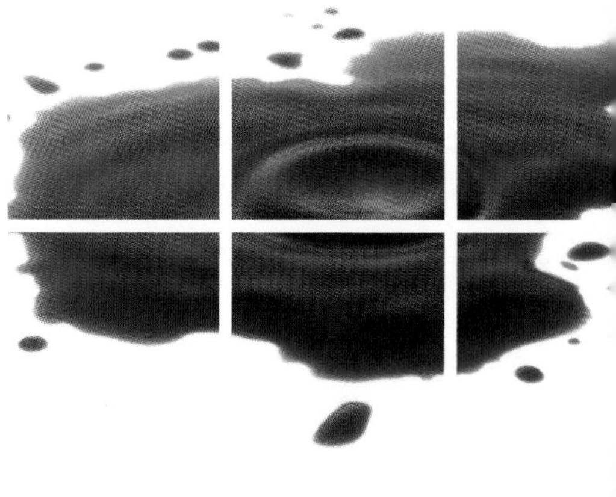

> Tip: If you're using powder blush directly on bare skin, be sure to powder your face first to prevent it from looking splotchy.

bronzer

are used to give the skin a warm, healthy glow. They usually come in powder and crème.

BRONZING POWDER. Like powder blush, it is the most popular because it's so easy to control and blend. It can come packaged in a variety of ways---pressed in a compact, loose in a tub, or even in a jar pressed into small balls or beads. Swiped across strategic areas of the face with a brush, it can bring the skin to life.

CRÈME BRONZERS are used just like bronzing powder to give the face a sun-kissed glow. You can find it in the form of a stick or even in compacts. It can be applied with your fingers or a sponge. It's great on dry skin, or when you don't want to wear foundation but want that little extra glow.

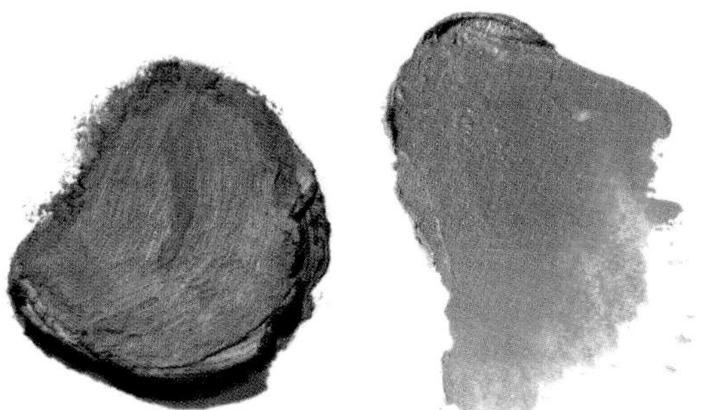

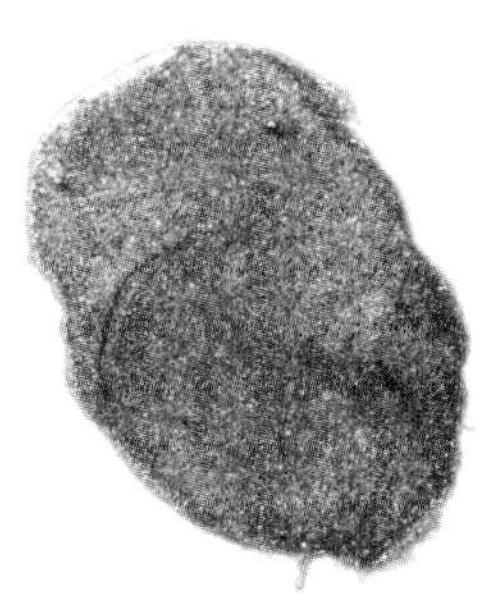

lipstick

is normally available in a variety of formulations.

MATTE delivers sophisticated and intense full-coverage color that contains absolutely no shine. Because of its formulation it stays on longer, but it can be drying and may give your lips the feeling and appearance of being dehydrated. It is great in dark, intense shades because it stays put and won't smear, but it certainly does nothing to make the lips look younger or fuller.

CRÈME contains more emollients than matte lipstick and provides a full coverage of moist though not shiny color. Most cosmetic lines offer the largest selection in this formula because it is the most versatile and popular. It wears quite well without being as dehydrating as matte.

FROST provides a pale, shiny, metallic appearance. But because of the single color of sheen in the formula's ingredients, there is a tendency for the lips to appear a little dry. It usually gives very opaque coverage that's not wonderful for mature lips.

SHEER is actually a glossy, sheer color-wash that allows the natural lips to show through because it is not formulated to cover opaquely. It's similar to a gel blush because it is simply pigments mixed with a gel. It lasts longer than a gloss but not as long as a crème lipstick. It's terrific for a quick fix because due to its sheerness it doesn't have to be applied with exact precision.

GLOSS is a lip color with extreme shine and moisture. It delivers a sheer layer of color that is going to need frequent reapplication. Although it doesn't last too terribly long, gloss gives a fresh-and-alive look that's perfect for all age groups. Used correctly it can make the lips look fuller and sexier. You'll find it packaged in a wand, tube or pot.

LIPLINER is a pencil that's used to define your lips. It helps correct lip shapes as well as prevent lip color from bleeding into fine lines. It can also be used over the entire lip then topped with a color. Using a lipliner greatly improves the staying power of any lip color.

The tools you use while applying your makeup can, in and of themselves, make a huge difference in its final result. Tools include everything from your choice of a sponge to your brushes to your powder puff. In this chapter I will identify some of these tools and identify basic applications for each. Remember that just as with makeup, there are no absolute rules, so you may use them in whichever way you choose to help achieve your desired effect.

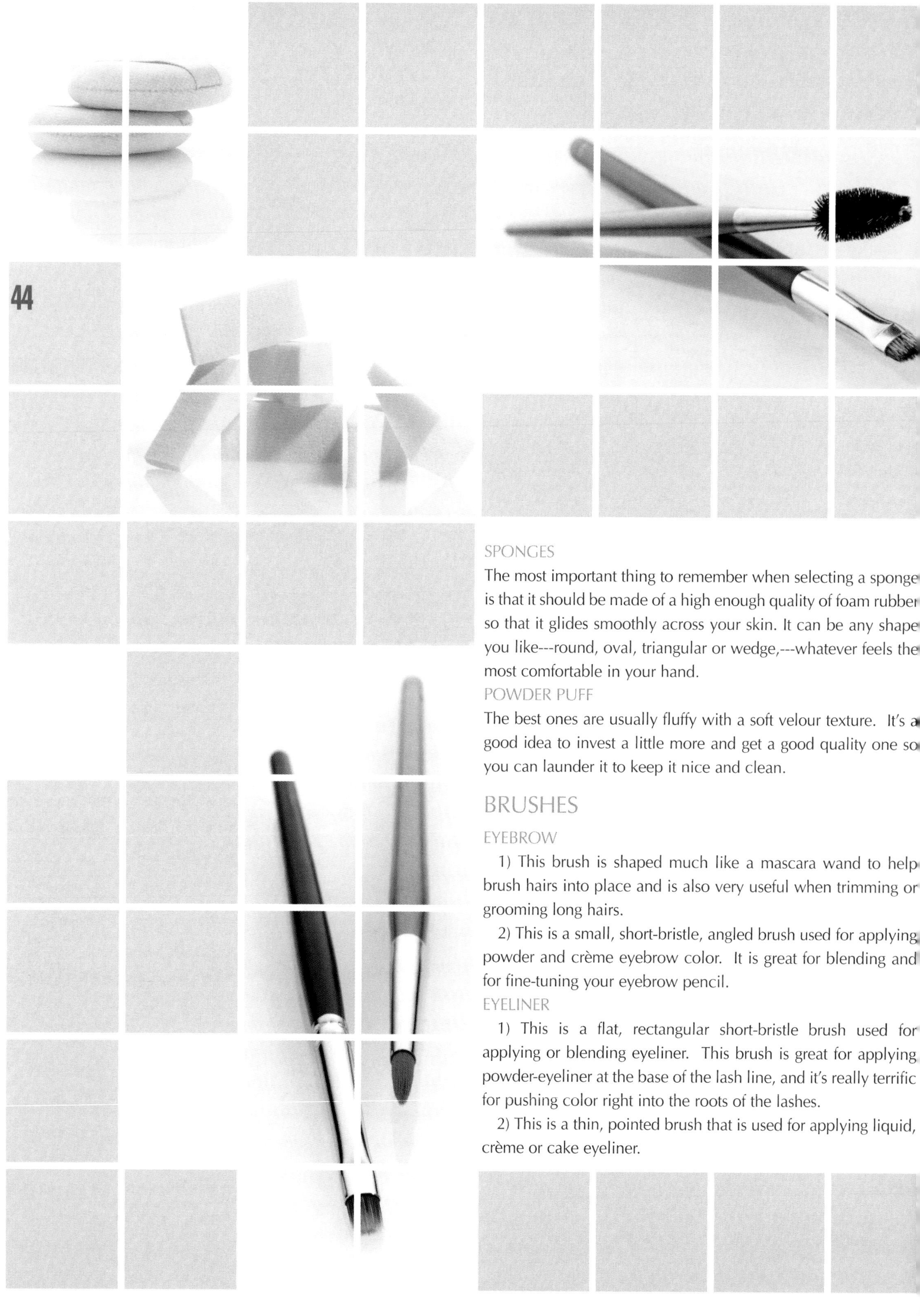

SPONGES

The most important thing to remember when selecting a sponge is that it should be made of a high enough quality of foam rubber so that it glides smoothly across your skin. It can be any shape you like---round, oval, triangular or wedge,---whatever feels the most comfortable in your hand.

POWDER PUFF

The best ones are usually fluffy with a soft velour texture. It's a good idea to invest a little more and get a good quality one so you can launder it to keep it nice and clean.

BRUSHES

EYEBROW

1) This brush is shaped much like a mascara wand to help brush hairs into place and is also very useful when trimming or grooming long hairs.

2) This is a small, short-bristle, angled brush used for applying powder and crème eyebrow color. It is great for blending and for fine-tuning your eyebrow pencil.

EYELINER

1) This is a flat, rectangular short-bristle brush used for applying or blending eyeliner. This brush is great for applying powder-eyeliner at the base of the lash line, and it's really terrific for pushing color right into the roots of the lashes.

2) This is a thin, pointed brush that is used for applying liquid, crème or cake eyeliner.

EYESHADOW

1) This is a short, round brush whose bristles have been cut at an angle. It can be used to apply your mid-tone colors or for blending. It also works very well for subtle crease color application.

2) This is a short, pointed brush that is perfect for smudging a lashline, or perhaps for adding more dramatic detail to your crease.

3) This is a tapered, oval-ended brush used to apply and blend contour color. It's also terrific for blending at the lashline, both top and bottom.

4) This is a long, thin, pointed brush that is used for applying mid-tone and definition color to the crease. It works great because its point is tapered so it begins to blend as you apply your color. This particular brush is fabulous for defining a crease that is barely there.

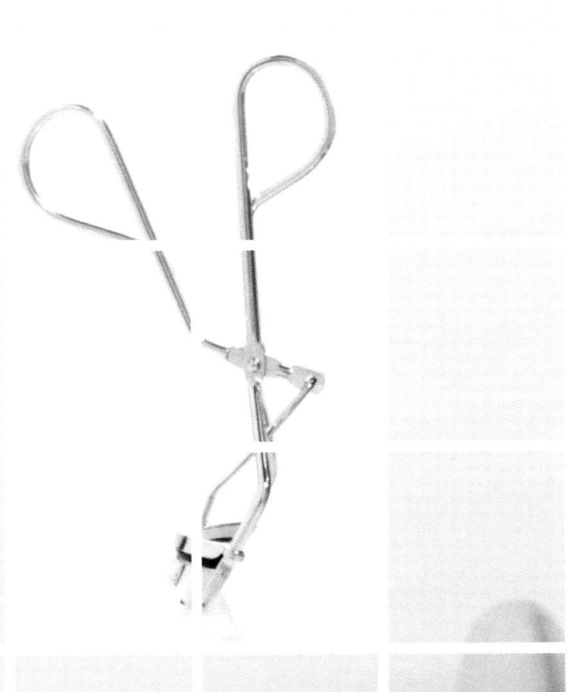

BLUSH (Opposite page)

This is a full, soft brush that can be used to apply either blush or bronzer.

EYELASH CURLER

This is a tool used to curl the lashes which in turn gives the illusion of "opening up" the eye.

FOUNDATION

This is a brush that is used to apply liquid or crème foundation. It's also great for touch-ups, or if you desire more coverage.

POWDER

This is a full, fluffy brush that is used to apply and blend face powder. It also works nicely for applying blush because it creates a soft, subtle effect.

CONCEALER

1) This is a small, pointed brush used when concealing small imperfections. It is effective for covering breakouts, broken capillaries and under-eye circles.

2) This is a flat, slightly tapered brush that is used to apply concealer to larger areas of discoloration.

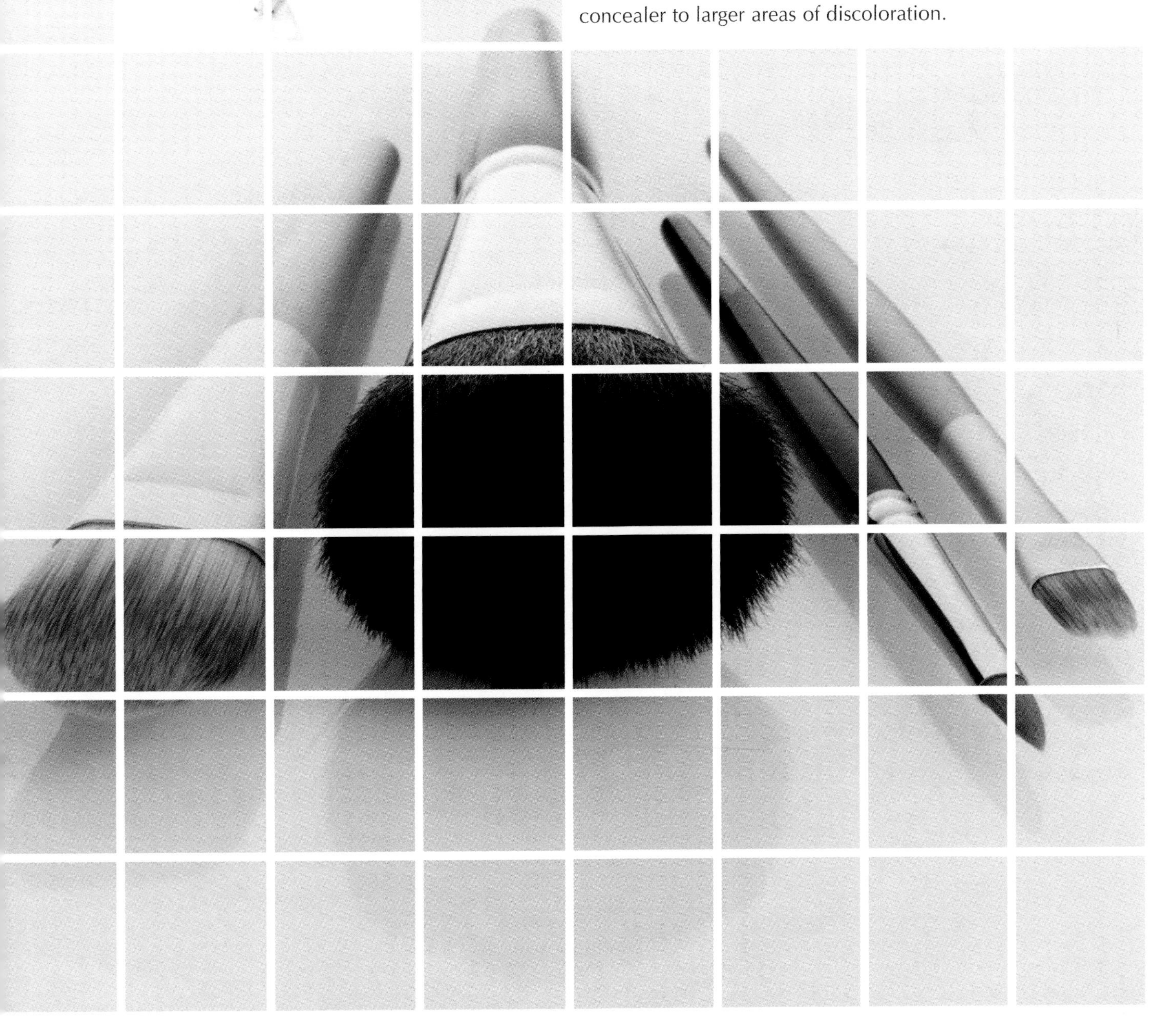

48

	shimmer	flesh	highlight
	shimmer	beige	highlight
	shimmer	gold	highlight
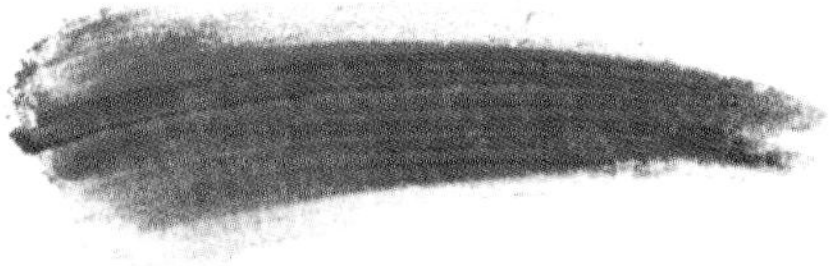	matte	taupe	midtone
	matte	dark taupe	midtone
	matte	mahogany	midtone
	shimmer	golden brown	contour
	shimmer	dark brown	contour
	matte	burgundy	contour
	matte	black	contour

eyeshadows

With respect to keeping it simple, I chose a very basic eyeshadow palette to use. With this palette, you can paint the eyes of women with any skin tone. Certainly there are thousands of eyeshadow colors you can use, but with just about every eye-shape you will want a highlight, midtone and contour color. It is the use of the three depth levels of color that helps to give shape to the eyelid. In all the before-and-after photos in this book these were the shadows used to create each and every look. Here are the colors, a brief color description and the best placement use.

5 colorchoices

In this chapter my goal is to help you make educated choices in selecting your color products. Choosing the correct shade of foundation is so important since it can affect the overall look of your make-up, as can the wrong choice of eye shadow, blush and lipstick. Together we can increase your chances of making the correct choices. Let's start the education process with a little foundation history.

All through the1950's, until the late1970's, women were told that it was correct to choose the opposite of their natural skin tone for their foundation color. For example, if your skin had olive undertones you used a pink-based foundation, and if your undertones were pink you used an orange-toned foundation.

And then in the 1980's, women were informed that this was all wrong and they should match their skin's exact undertone. So if you had pink undertones your foundation color had to be pink-based. If your undertones were olive, you put on an olive-toned foundation---well, you get the picture.

Then finally in the 1990's, the cosmetic industry discovered that yellow undertones, instead of being undesirable, actually made the skin look the most alive and the most natural. So, in other words, practically everyone looks better with some yellow in their foundation.

skinchart

Let's try to make this simple.

There are approximately 15 levels of depth to the skin. "Depth" is the lightness or darkness of your skin, Level 1 being very pale (porcelain) and Level 15 being very dark (ebony). At each level there is a basic undertone that is needed to make your skin look its best.

85% of women's skin varies in different tones of "warm". In my opinion, warmer skin always looks more youthful. Only about 15% of women are truly "cool". They usually have dark hair, pale skin and light eyes.

One of the biggest makeup mistakes women make is in thinking they have cool undertones when they don't. The following chart is to help you better understand depth levels of skin and what is needed to improve its appearance.

tone	depth level	shade needed
fair	1	
fair	2	
fair	3	
medium	4	
medium	5	
medium	6	
olive	7	
olive	8	
olive	9	
bronze	10	
bronze	11	
light ebony	12	
light ebony	13	
light ebony	14	
dark ebony	15	

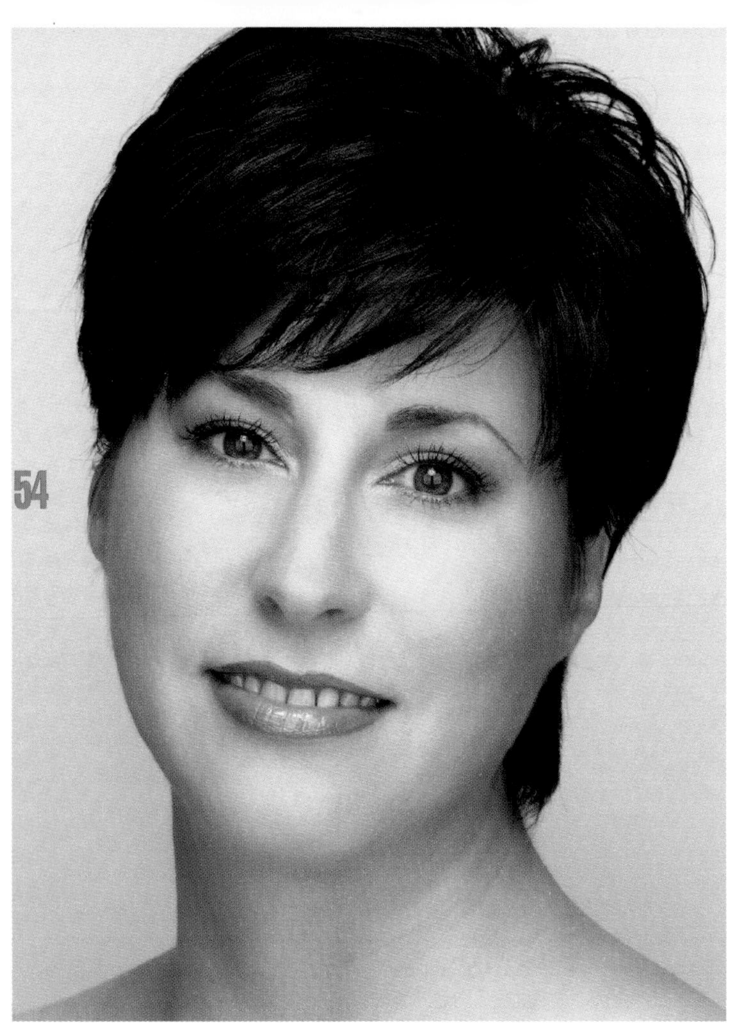

rhonda shasteen

SKIN LEVEL: 2 (fair)
FACE SHAPE: pear-shaped face
EYE SHAPE: close-set eyes
SHADOWS: Highlight-shimmer flesh
Midtone-matte taupe
Contour-shimmer golden brown
OBJECTIVE: to give the illusion of a more oval-shaped face. To visually pull the eyes apart.
APPLICATION: contoured the jawline and cheeks to minimize their width. Highlighted the forehead to create the illusion of more width. Highlighted the inner corner of eyelids to visually push the eyes apart. Defined the outer corners of eyes with the deepest shadow.

sherril steinman

SKIN LEVEL: 3 (fair)
FACE SHAPE: pear-shaped face
EYE SHAPE: hooded eyes
SHADOWS: Highlight-shimmer beige
Midtone-matte taupe/ matte dark taupe
Contour-shimmer dark brown
OBJECTIVE: to give the illusion of a more oval-shaped face. To minimize the hooded appearance of the eyelids, making her eyes to appear more open.
APPLICATION: contoured the jawline and cheeks to minimize their width. Highlighted the forehead to create the illusion of more width. Using midtone and contour colors, applied, then blended them to the hooded area, giving the illusion that the area recedes.

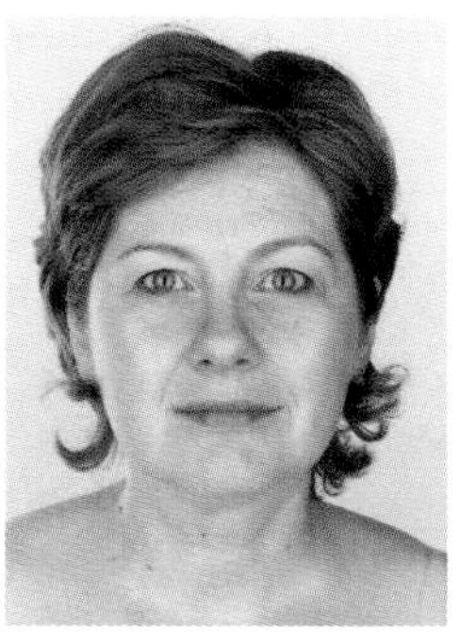

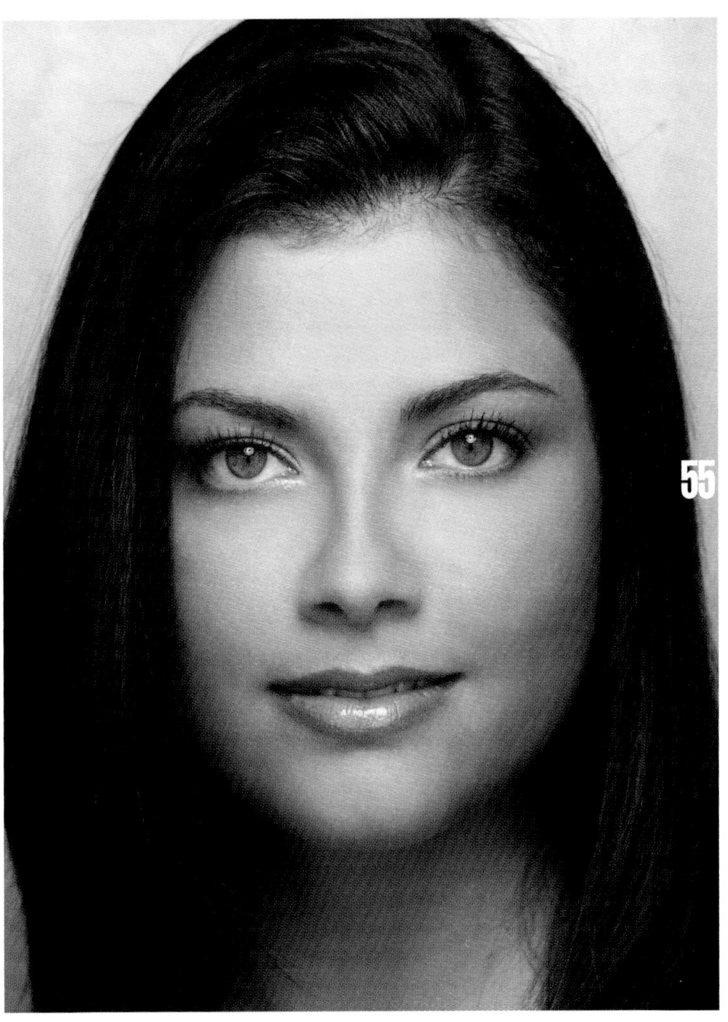

linda bird

SKIN LEVEL: 5 (medium)
FACE SHAPE: pear-shaped face

SHADOWS: Highlight-shimmer beige
Midtone-matte taupe
Contour-shimmer dark brown

OBJECTIVE: to give the illusion of a more oval-shaped face.
APPLICATION: contoured the jawline and cheeks to minimize their width. Highlighted forehead to create the illusion of more width. Highlighted the eyelid to brighten the eye, then concentrated on defining the crease and the lashline.

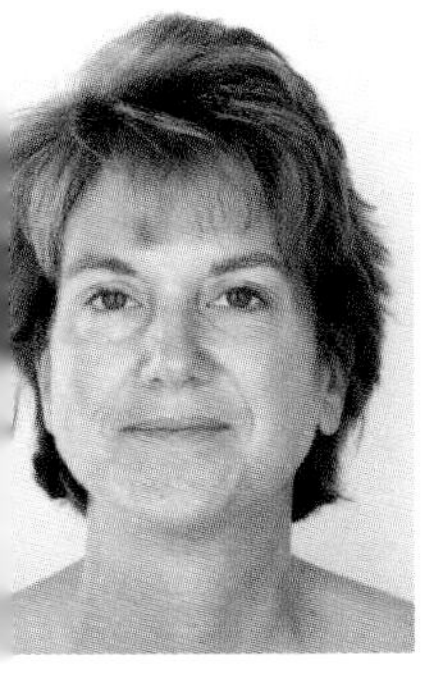

michelle boye

SKIN LEVEL: 6 (medium)
FACE SHAPE: square-shaped face
EYE SHAPE: wide-set eyes
SHADOWS: Highlight-shimmer beige
Midtone-matte dark taupe
Contour-shimmer dark brown

OBJECTIVE: to give the illusion of a more oval-shaped face. To help it appear as if the eyes are closer together.
APPLICATION: contoured hairline and jawline to soften the "four corners". Highlighted down the center of the forehead, nose and chin. Applied a darker midtone to the inside hollow of her eyes, to visually pull the eye placement closer together.

eleanor simon

SKIN LEVEL: 7 (olive)
FACE SHAPE: oval-shaped face
EYE SHAPE: hooded eye
SHADOWS: Highlight-shimmer beige
Midtone-matte taupe/matte dark taupe
Contour-shimmer golden brown
OBJECTIVE: to minimize the hooded appearance of the eyelids, causing her eyes to appear more open and alive.
APPLICATION: applied midtone and contour color to the hooded area of the lids to help them recede and "open up" the eyes. Subtly layered color, starting with light and increasing to dark taupe, to the hooded area so as to create a more natural effect.

lydia duron

SKIN LEVEL: 8 (olive)
FACE SHAPE: square-shaped face
EYE SHAPE: hooded eyes
SHADOWS: Highlight-shimmer beige
Midtone-matte dark taupe
Contour-shimmer dark brown
OBJECTIVE: to give the illusion of a more oval-shaped face. To minimize the hooded appearance of her eyelids, causing her eyes to appear more open and alive.
APPLICATION: contoured the hairline and jaw to soften the "four corners". Highlighted down the center of the forehead, nose and the tip of the chin. Subtly layered color to the hooded areas to help minimize them. (Really beautiful brows are important with hooded eyes because they will draw attention up and away.)

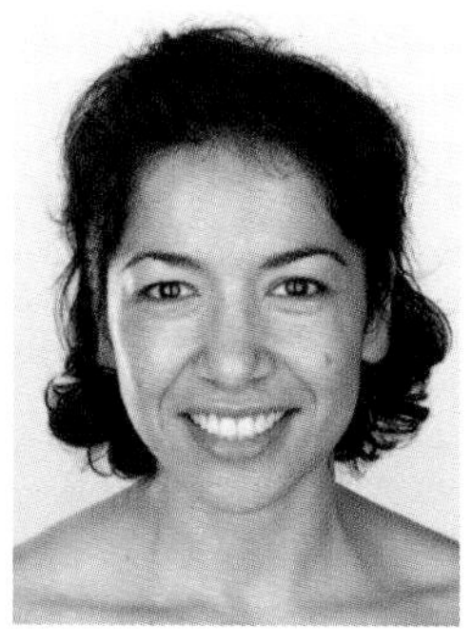

sonja hunter mason

SKIN LEVEL: 12 (light ebony)
FACE SHAPE: round-shaped face
EYE SHAPE: wide-set eyes
SHADOWS: Highlight-shimmer gold
Midtone-matte mahogany
Contour-dark burgundy

OBJECTIVE: to give the illusion of a more oval-shaped face. To even out skin tone and brighten areas to add life to the face.
APPLICATION: Using multiple shades of foundation, evened out skin tone then highlighted areas with a golden-orange face powder to give life to the skin. Softly sculpted her cheeks, jaw and temples. Highlight the lid and contoured the inside hollow of eyes to visually pull them closer.

alischia butler

SKIN LEVEL: 15 (dark ebony)
FACE SHAPE: square-shaped face

SHADOWS: Highlight-shimmer gold
Midtone-matte mahogany
Contour-dark burgundy

OBJECTIVE: to give the illusion of a more oval-shaped face. To even out skin tone and brighten areas to add life to the face.
APPLICATION: using multiple shades of foundation, evened out the slight skin discoloration. The main goal was to brighten her face. Which was achieved by using a golden-orange face powder to highlight areas. Contoured hairline and jaw to soften the "four corners".

foundation

As you can see from the skin chart (see page 53), for the most part some shade of yellow works for just about all skin tones. The most natural looks reflect beige, neutral or yellow tones.

The only time you might need a foundation with slight pink undertones is at the very palest level because at that level pink works simply because it is a true pink, and not red. Pink undertones at any level darker than 2 are red---and no one wants a red face.

I can't emphasize enough that pink-based foundation and powder will make the skin look older.

A good thing to bear in mind is that relative to foundation, pink is red, and red undertones are always undesirable. Women who have a natural flush in their cheeks are sometimes tempted to buy a pink-based foundation to match. They should resist the temptation because yellow-based foundation will counteract the red, and we have already learned that pink on top of pink can give the skin an aged look.

Most Caucasian skin is either slightly yellow-toned or ruddy, so yellow will always help to minimize any red you might have from broken capillaries, tanning or aging. Yellow-based foundations will also tone down high coloring such as rosacea.

Often women who have strong, red undertones feel that yellow-toned foundations look too yellow. Given a little time on the skin they will absorb and adjust to the skin and will start to look natural.

Since yellow-based foundations work well on almost everyone, be sure to select a foundation that has yellow undertones. It's very flattering and it will effectively even out most complexions by blending very nicely into natural coloring.

Bear in mind that if your skin contains natural yellow undertones, you should definitely avoid foundations that are too white because they'll make you look chalky---even ashy. Most ethnic skin has strong yellow or golden undertones, so by all means embrace your natural yellow undertones.

There are a few extra considerations when choosing foundation for ebony skin. First, a large percentage of ebony women have what is called "facial masking". Facial masking refers to areas of darker pigmentation generally found on the outer perimeter of the face---usually along the jawline and across the forehead. If you have any degree of facial masking, you will probably need to use at least two shades of foundation to equalize your skin tone: one shade to brighten, another to deepen.

Secondly, with ebony skin it is very important to match the undertones exactly because they are so strong, distinct and noticeable. They range all the way from golden-orange to true brown. Keep in mind that it is always a good idea to try to brighten (not lighten) deep-toned ebony skin. God gave you plenty of pigment, so let's brighten your face and give it life. Intense golden-orange tones work really well for brightening your skin.

When selecting your foundation color, remember never to make a decision in artificial light because it can be very deceptive. One of the best ways to choose a foundation color is to do a "stripe test". Apply three stripes of different shades to your cheek or lower jawline, wait a few minutes to see if the oils in your skin will change the color pigments, then examine the stripes carefully to see which one best matches the depth of your skin. If you have pink or red undertones it's so important to wait a minute or two before you make your decision because the yellow will adjust to your complexion. If the depth of the shade you choose matches your neck, you've chosen correctly.

powder/concealer

For almost all the ethnic skin tones, concealer with a yellow undertone is the best color choice because it works for all skin imperfections. It counteracts the purple of under-eye circles as well as the brown of age-spots, and it covers any splotchy ruddiness or red in the complexion.

On ebony skin, golden-orange for lighter to medium skin tones works wonderfully. And on really deep tones of ebony a warm brown is usually best.

As with foundation and concealer, a face powder with a yellow undertone is the best choice. If you like, you can use two shades---one that matches your skin-tone level and the other, one level lighter, for use as a highlighter on areas such as under the eye, on the forehead, down the center of the nose and the middle of the chin. This works well and looks extremely natural.

This method is also especially effective on ebony skin. I generally use a golden-orange powder for highlighting ebony skin because it brightens the face. Most women-of-color already have a good deal of pigment in their skin so they will most often just want to brighten their faces rather than adding additional pigment. Additionally, with darker levels of powder you might find that a large number of them contain a slight sheen to prevent them from appearing ashy.

One other important point I would like to cover is that translucent powder is not invisible, even though the word might lead one to believe that it is. It is less opaque than other powders, but it's definitely not colorless and if you're not careful it can even make you look ashy.

eye color	liner	shadow
blue	warm brown/taupe	rich warm browns/ warm taupes
green	red-brown/taupe	golden browns/ warm taupes/ deep purples
brown	rich brown/ charcoal/taupe	golden brown/blue/ green/light mahogany/ charcoal/purple
grey	charcoal/deep brown	charcoal/cool brown/ purple

eyeshadow

When choosing eye-shadow colors there are two very important things to remember. The first is the tone of your skin. Naturally, you'll want to make sure the shades you select always complement your skin-tone. But probably the most important thing to remember when choosing the shade of your eye shadow is your eye color, because the objective is to "bring it out"---make it pop.

The most effective way to make eye color more vibrant is to surround it with a contrasting shade.

Here is a chart that will give you some suggestions of shades that work well with your eye color.

Eyeliner:

The most effective eyeliner color choices for defining and correcting eye shapes are taupe, brown and black. Pastel and colored eyeliners are not particularly effective with eye definition, but they can help pop the eye color.

blush

The goal is to find a blush color that's natural and neutral but still brightens and adds life to the face. Notice how your skin looks after a jog around the block or when you blush naturally. When you flush it registers on the skin as a shade of pink. It could be a deep pink, a soft rose or even a warm, tanned peachy color for those with warmer skin tones. Whichever the hue, the base is usually a shade of pink. Even ebony skin looks fabulous with a deep bronzy pink. Please remember that with blush the goal is to brighten the face.

lips

I have created a chart that will assist you when you are choosing lip shades. Just remember that the most important factor to keep in mind is your skin tone. Since your goal is to make your face look vibrant and alive, it really makes a difference in how the color works.

skintones	lipsticks
fair	glossy, transparent pinks/soft peach/ honey brown/beige brown/soft berry
medium	warm pinks/soft mocha/carmel/ delicate red/warm apricots/tangy peach
olive	strong red/deep rose/berry/toffee/ mahogany/rich warm apricots/brown red
ebony	deep brownish red/deep berry/ deep fushia/golden beige

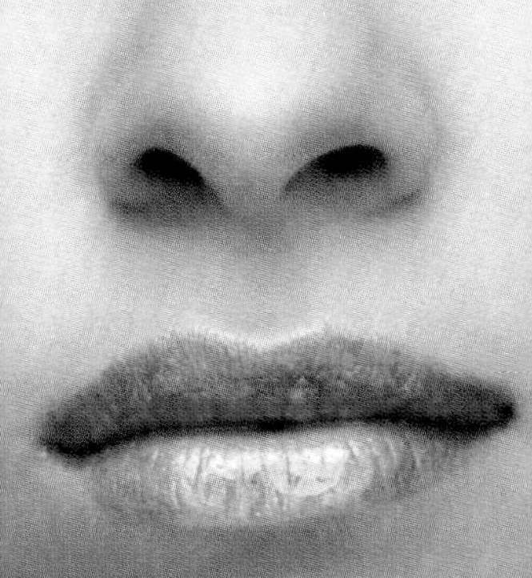

6 faceshape

Although there are no set hard-and-fast rules to makeup, there are definitely some do's and don'ts that apply to the different facial shapes. Feel free to experiment and try new things. It's only makeup---you can always wash it off and start over.

susan t. billy

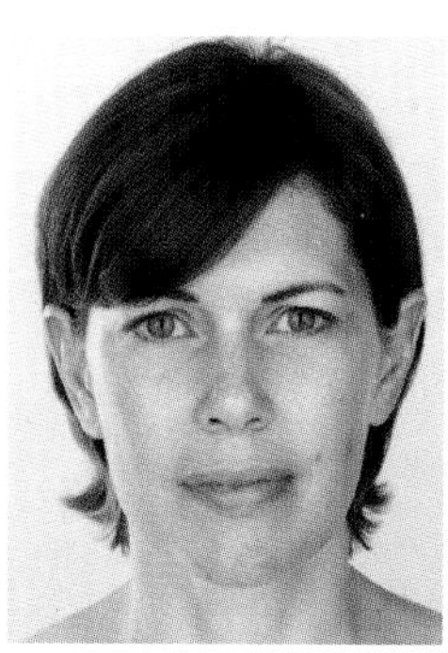

ovalface

An oval shaped face is considered by most to be the perfect facial shape because of its beautiful symmetry. It is usually broader at the cheeks, tapering in slightly at both the forehead and the chin. Because of its symmetry you can play all you want. An oval face can support most makeup trends---so have fun.

carol aaron

roundface

A round shaped face is fuller and generally holds its youthful appearance longer than the other shapes. It's shorter, fairly wide, with full cheeks and a rounded chin.

Most women who feel they have a full face mistakenly think they have a round face, but in reality, it usually is not.

If you have a round shaped face:

**Don't just wear blush on the apples of the cheeks because it will further shorten and widen the face.

**Softly sculpt your cheeks, jaw and temples with a product such as a bronzer, pressed powder or a foundation that is one to two levels darker than your skin tone. Then apply the color of your choice to the apples of your cheeks.

**Don't kohl-rim your eyes with a dark liner because it will make them look smaller and more isolated on the face.

**Elongate your eye shadow up because it will "pull" the eyes up and give your face a slightly longer appearance.

Brow Box: Your brows can also help shape your face so if you have a round shaped face taper your brows outward toward the tips of the ears (not down) because this also will help with the illusion of lengthening the face.

arlene lenarz

squareface

I personally consider this shape to be one of the most beautiful and one of the most photogenic because it suggests strength, and the features are usually symmetrically balanced. A square-shaped face is usually the same width at the forehead, the cheeks and the jaw.

If you have a square-shaped face:

**Highlight down the center of the forehead, nose and the tip of the chin to draw attention to the middle of the face.

**Contour your hairline and jaw with a product that is slightly darker than your skin-tone to soften the overall appearance.

**Blush the apples of the cheeks. This draws attention away from the corners of the square; it will widen that area and make it appear slightly more oval.

> Brow Box: With a square-shaped face, curve the brows down toward the middle of the ear to minimize the width of the forehead.

kathy peel

heart-shapedface

The heart-shaped face is wide at the forehead and curves down to a pointed or narrow chin.

If you have a heart-shaped face:

**Highlight your chin. Highlighting it will broaden its width and make it look less pointed.

**Contour your temples and define the hollows of your cheeks to diminish the width of this portion of your face.

**Strengthen the eyes or the lips---but not both---to increase definition and divert attention from the wider areas.

Tip: Pressed powder works well for sculpting the face because it's low in pigment and blends easily---or if you like, you could use a bronzer; just be sure to blend really well.

Brow Box: For a heart-shaped face, ideally your brows should taper towards the tip of your ears to help lengthen your face.

karen piro

pear-shapedface

The pear-shaped face is narrow at the temples and forehead and wider at the jawline.

If you have a pear-shaped face:

** Highlight the forehead to create the illusion of width.

** Contour the jawline and cheeks to minimize their width.

Brow Box: For a pear-shaped face, extend the brow slightly beyond the outer corner of the eye, being sure not to make your arch too extreme. Extending the brow out will give the illusion of width.

Tip: Remember that the proper hairstyle can go a long way in balancing any facial shape.

michelle muslin

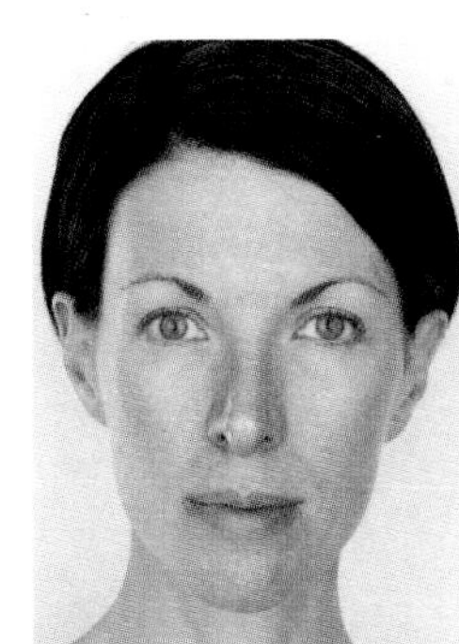

longface

The long shaped face has high cheekbones, a high, deep forehead and a strong, sharp, chiseled jawline.

If you have a long face:

**Don't sculpt your face because it will tend to lengthen it even more.

**Apply blush to the apples of your cheeks because this will shorten and widen the face.

Tip: When applying your blush, start closer in on the apples of the cheeks and brush outward across the face.

Brow Box: On a long face, don't make your eyebrow arch too extreme---a straighter or more gently curved brow will widen the face.

Before you begin to apply makeup, there is some preparation work to be done that we will discuss in this chapter. Although doing it might seem a little tedious, if you skip it, your finished makeup won't be as beautiful or as polished as it could have been.

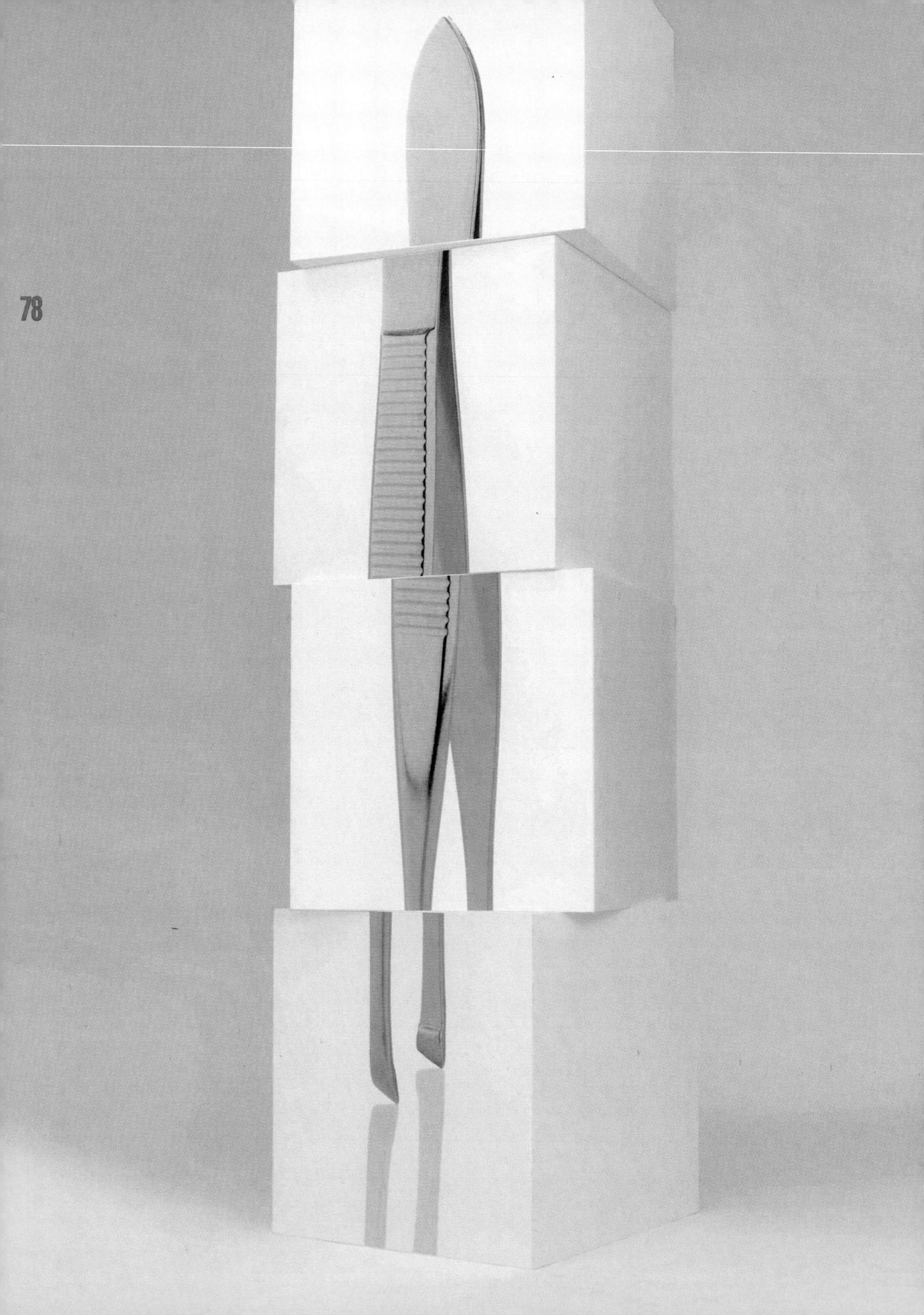

browattack

Grooming your eyebrows is an absolute must.
Let me start by saying that you should embrace your natural brow-shape. It is important to remember not to try to make your eyebrows do something they can't. Some people have brows that grow in a gentle curve rather than a definite arch, while others, grow naturally straighter across the face.

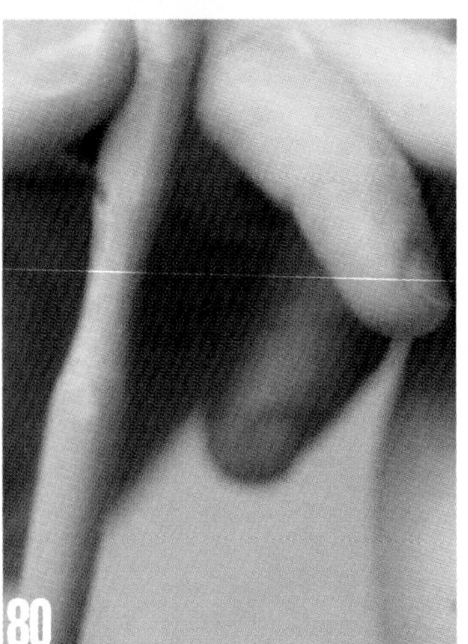

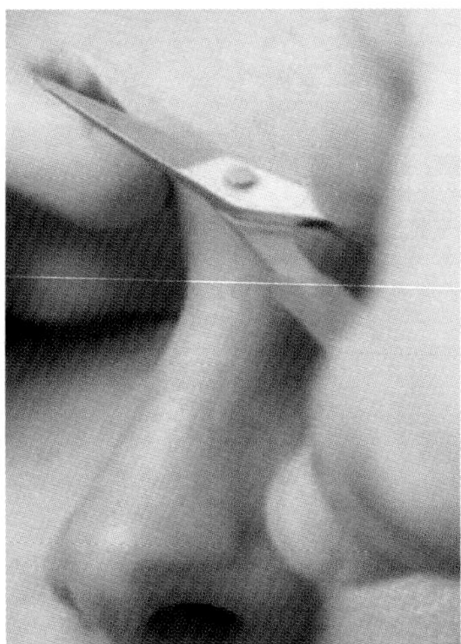
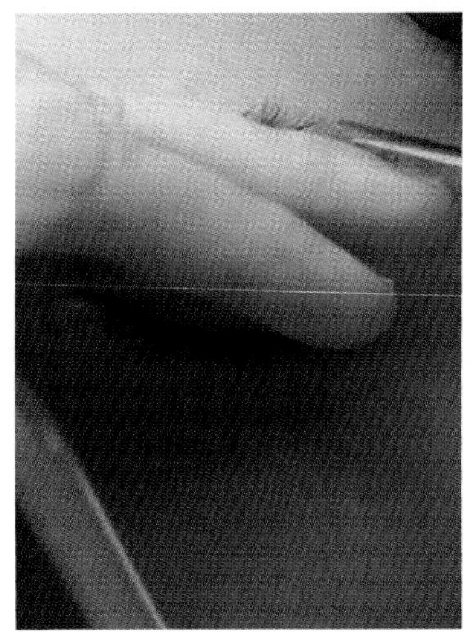

Before we begin, gather your tools together. You will need a pair of tweezers, a brow brush, a small pair of scissors and a white eye-pencil.

Now let's evaluate your brows.

First, are they too dense? Eyebrows that are too dense can be softened either by trimming them or lightening the color.

To trim them, simply brush them up and snip any stray hairs that extend past the upper brow line. Next, brush them down, and snip any unruly hairs that extend past the lower brow line.

Many times brow hairs are actually longer than they appear because the tips of the hairs are light in color and when they reach a certain length they tend to curl. By trimming them, you trim away some of the density and that slight curl so that the hairs lay down more neatly.

It's important to remember that if you need to trim your brows it should be done before you start to tweeze. Otherwise you might ruin your brow-line by tweezing away hairs that should have stayed but were simply too long.

Are your brows too pale, or are they speckled with gray? If they are, you might choose to have them tinted. It will help define them and alleviate the need for as much eyebrow makeup.

Now it's tweeze-time.

The best time to tweeze your brow is when your skin is softer after a steamy shower. It's a lot less painful because your pores are already open. Try to tweeze in natural light --you can see what you're doing so much better.

After plucking a couple of hairs from one brow, move to the other, then back and forth a few hairs at a time to guard the symmetry. Always tweeze in the same direction as the hair grows or the hair might not grow back lying properly.

HOW DO YOU DETERMINE WHERE TO START?

The information here will help you know where your brow should start and stop and approximately where it should arch.

Holding a pencil vertically against the side of your nose, notice where it meets the brow. That is where your brow should begin.

Next, hold the pencil against your nostril and diagonally across the pupil of your eye. Notice where it meets the brow. That is probably the best place for the peak of your arch.

Then, still with the pencil lying against your nostril, extend it diagonally to your eye's outer corner. Where it meets the brow is the best place for your brow to end.

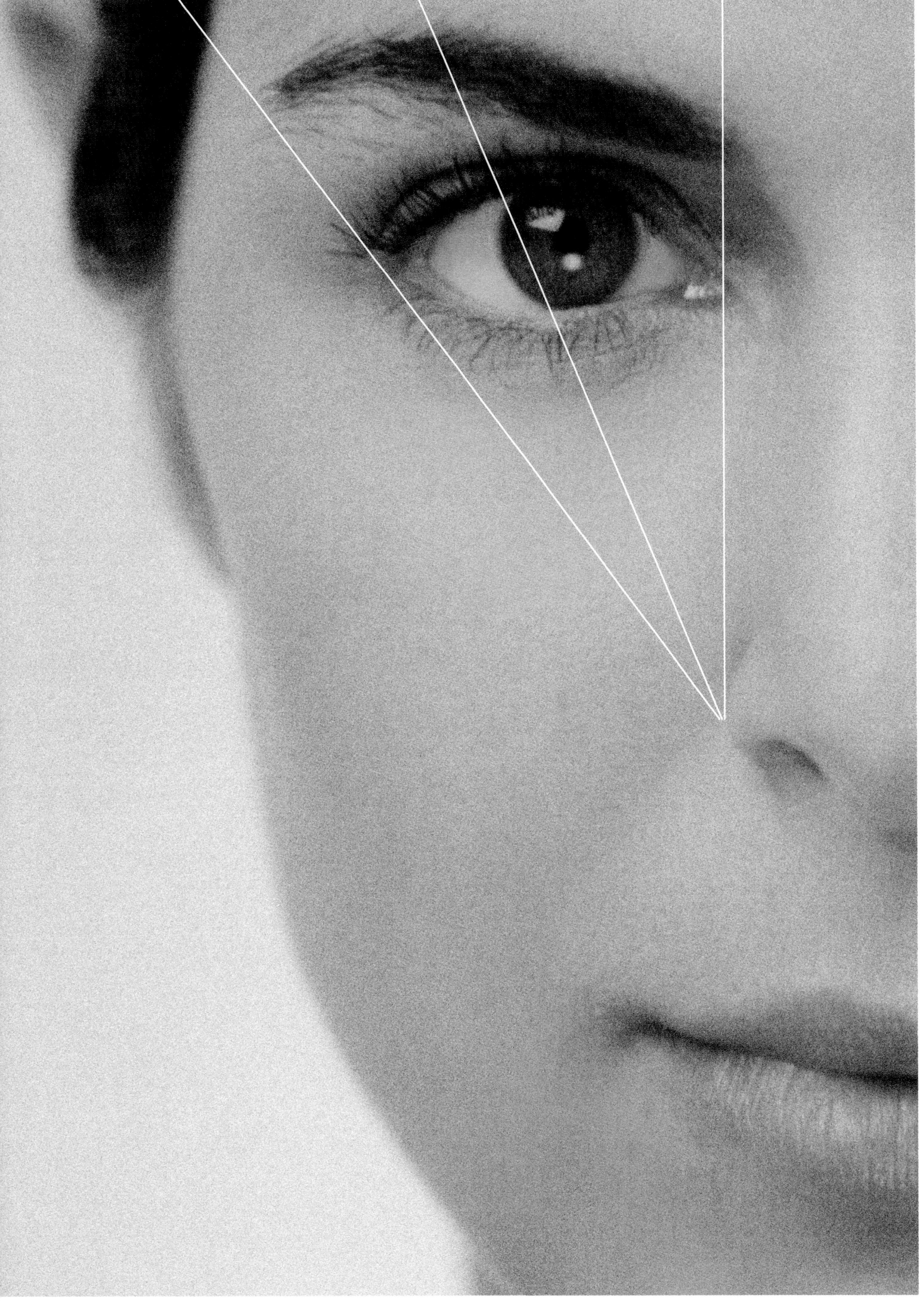

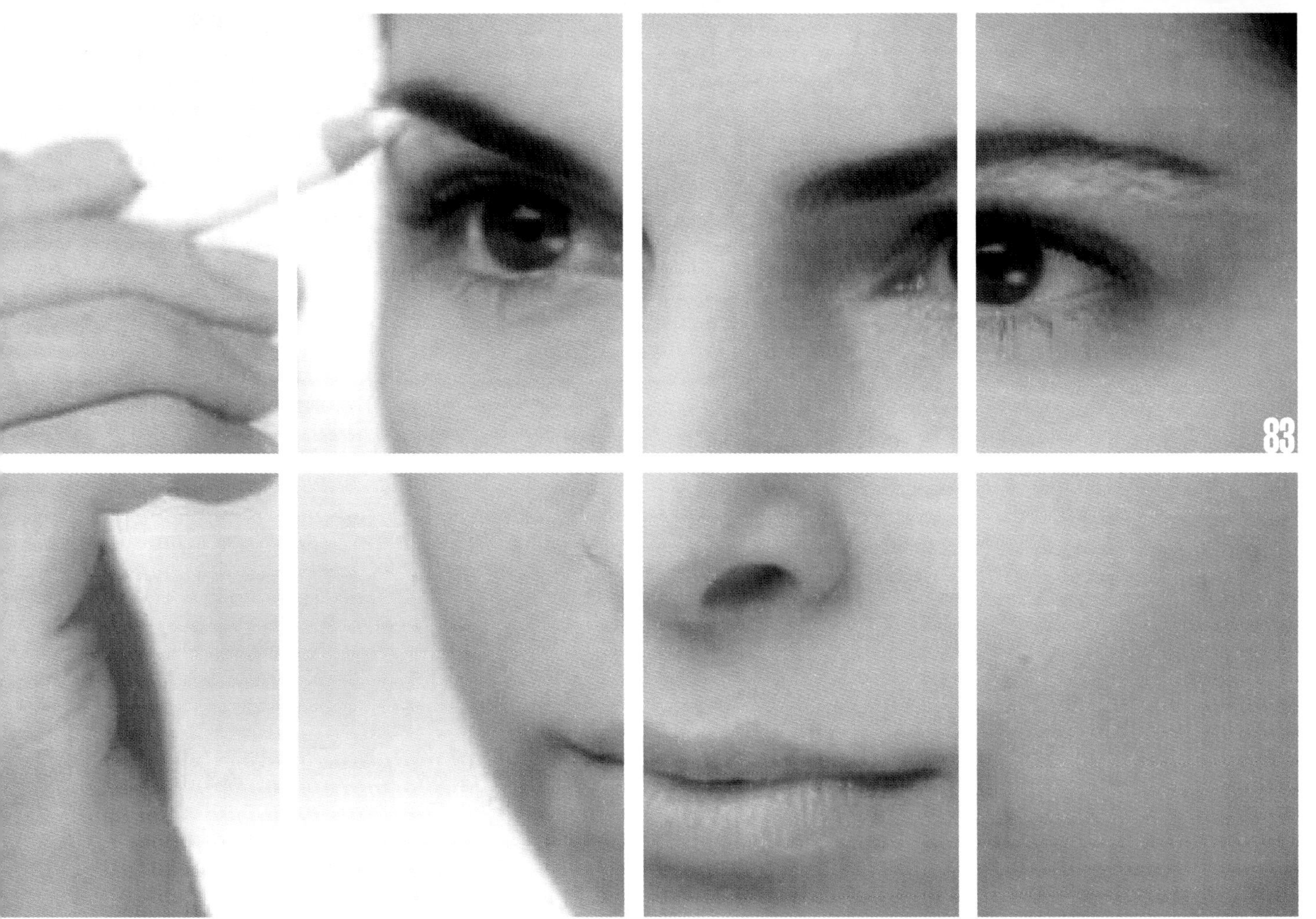

A great trick when preparing to tweeze is to use a white eye pencil to sketch a pattern-outline (a template of sorts) of the shape you want your brow to be. This is a great way to get a preview of the end result before you actually do the tweezing. It's then a simple matter of removing only the hairs that are covered with the white.

Tip: Take care not to overdo it because sparse brows, especially on a mature face, will make for a harder and older look.

Tip: You can wax unwanted hairs, but be aware that the hairs may not grow back lying down correctly because wax is pulled off in the opposite direction of the hairs' growth. Also, a quick note; waxing repeatedly may eventually cause a crepe-like appearance to the skin.

moisturizer

Moisturizing is an important step that helps your foundation go on smoothly and evenly.

Make sure to begin with a freshly washed face, then apply your moisturizer. It's best applied to a damp face because it goes on more evenly. Moisturizer evens the skin's porosity and is most effective when it's left to absorb for a few minutes before you apply your makeup. You can use a light moisturizer or a heavy one; just make sure you choose the right one for your particular skin type.

Moisturizers for normal skin are usually light to help even out any dry areas.

Moisturizers for dry skin are usually higher in emollients and are richer.

Moisturizers for sensitive skin are fragrance and irritant free.

Moisturizer for oily skin is extremely light so as not to clog the pores. If you're wondering why oily skin would ever need moisturizer, it's because oily skin can be over-dried by cleansers. The skin combats this by producing more and more oils, which can cause the complexion to look greasy. By applying a little light moisturizer you can help the skin from producing more oil, and help even its porosity.

Tip: Never apply moisturizer to the eyelids because it will cause your eye shadows to crease and not last as long.

primer

Using primer is not an absolute must, but since it's longer-wearing than moisturizer it can help your skin stay fresher longer. The purpose of a primer is to even out the skin's porosity and help the foundation go on smoothly, evenly and stay on longer. Primer helps to prevent your foundation color from altering due to your skin's natural oils because it creates a barrier between those natural oils and your foundation. Simply apply it on top of your moisturizer before you apply your foundation.

exfoliate

Your lips should be exfoliated regularly. A great time to do it is right after your shower. Apply a generous amount of lip balm then wait a few minutes for it to absorb. Using a soft bristle toothbrush brush your lips vigorously then reapply more lip balm. If you prefer you could use your towel to rub your lips. But whichever method you use, always moisturize when you've finished.

Tip: Moisturizing lips before applying lipstick will help your lip color go on more smoothly.

The four basic skin types are provided on the following pages. I have listed them with their characteristics to help you decipher your particular skin type.

Also listed are the foundation formulas that work well with each skin type. This will help you make an educated decision when selecting your foundation.

skintype	characteristics	needs	best foundation (texture)
dry	usually mature skin/ lacks emoillents/ less elastic/ rarely breakout/ feels tight after cleansing/ usually small pores	moisturizing foundations/ formula containing emollients and anti-oxidents	tinted (moisturizer)/ liquid (moisturizing)/ mousse
ormal	few to no breakouts/ neither to oily nor to dry/ medium pores/ smooth and even texture/ healthy color	ph balanced products	cream to powder/ tinted (moisturizer)/ liquid (all types)/ cream/ dual finish/ stick/ mousse
oily	prone to blackheads/ large pores/ get shiny fast/ breakout often/ wrinkles less/ usually highly elastic	oil-free products/ noncomedogenic/ products enrich with oil absorbers	cream to powder/ liquid (oil-free) (water-based)/ dual finish/ mousse
ensitive	burns easily (very)/ blotchy and dry patches/ more susceptible to rosacea/ sensitive to many products/ flush easily/ thin, delicate	hypo allergenic/ fragrance free moisturizing formulas/ formulas without chemical sunscreens	liquid (water-based)/ mousse/ tinted (moisturizer)/ dual finish

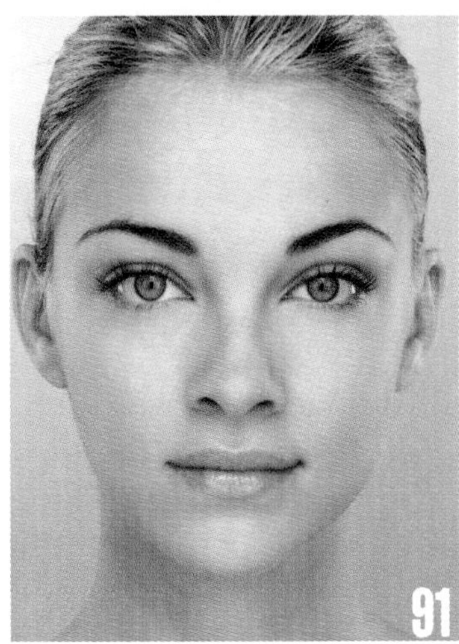

applying foundation

FOUNDATION

Selecting a foundation that's perfect for you will probably be your most difficult decision.

All the information I've given you so far will help make it easier.

In addition, ask yourself these four questions. The answers should lead you to the correct decision.

1. What is my skin-type?
2. What color undertones are in my skin?
3. How much coverage do I want?
4. What type of finish do I want?

The finish is very important because certain finishes work better on some skin textures than they do on others.

**MATTE works best on skin with imperfections such as breakouts, scars and discoloration. It gives you the best coverage, and it's perfect for oily skin because it contains no oils. However, use a light hand because if you apply it too heavily it can appear mask-like.

**DEWY looks youthful and is wonderful on most skin types with the exception of oily skin. It will, unfortunately, showcase any flaw such as surface bumps and blemishes.

**SATIN gives the skin a soft, smooth appearance. The finish is not as flat as matte or as shiny as dewy but between the two.

**LUMINOUS works well on any skin type. Its light-reflecting properties help hide tiny flaws and lines by reflecting light off the surface of the face.

When applying foundation you have three basic tools at your disposal.

•A sponge, which is the most sanitary because you can wash it or just throw it away. Sponges also really help with the blending process.

•A brush blends well so it's great for touching up the foundation you've had on all day.

•Don't have a brush or a sponge handy? Mislaid them? No problem because the third tool is your fingertips. Fingers work well because they warm the foundation---and you always know where to find them!

BASIC

It's best to begin your application on the center of the face, dotting foundation on the cheeks and the forehead then blending outward. Always remember to finish by blending downward to make sure all the small facial hairs lay flat. After application, blot with a tissue to absorb any oils left from the product. This will really help the staying power of your foundation. And don't forget to apply a light coat to the eyelids because it will make your eye-shadow glide on more easily and stay on longer.

> Tip: The best way to achieve a natural look is to first go all over the face with a sheer foundation, then go back and dot your concealer on any small imperfections.

> Tip: Foundation can also be applied to your lips. It creates a blank canvas for any reshaping you want or need to do. It's also useful as an anchor for lipstick since it helps it stay on longer.

elaine moock

SKIN LEVEL: 3 (fair)
FACE SHAPE: square-shaped face
EYE SHAPE: hooded eyes
SHADOWS: Highlight-shimmer flesh
Midtone-matte taupe
Contour-matte dark taupe
OBJECTIVE: to give the illusion of a more oval-shaped face. To minimize the hooded appearance of her eyelids making the eyes to appear more open and alive.
APPLICATION: contoured hairline and jaw to soften the "four corners". Highlighted down the center of the forehead, nose, and the tip of the chin. Layered midtone and contour colors on hooded areas. The layering of color will help the end result look more subtle and natural.

pat smith

SKIN LEVEL: 10 (bronze)
FACE SHAPE: square-shaped face

SHADOWS: Highlight-shimmer gold
Midtone-matte mahogany
Contour-matte mahogany
OBJECTIVE: to give the illusion of a more oval-shaped face.
APPLICATION: contoured the hairline and jaw to soften the "four corners". Highlighted down the center of the forehead, nose, and tip of the chin. Highlighted the lid and brow bone. To create the definition at the lashline and in the crease, chose to layer the midtone color rather than a darker color.

kerrie bodrato

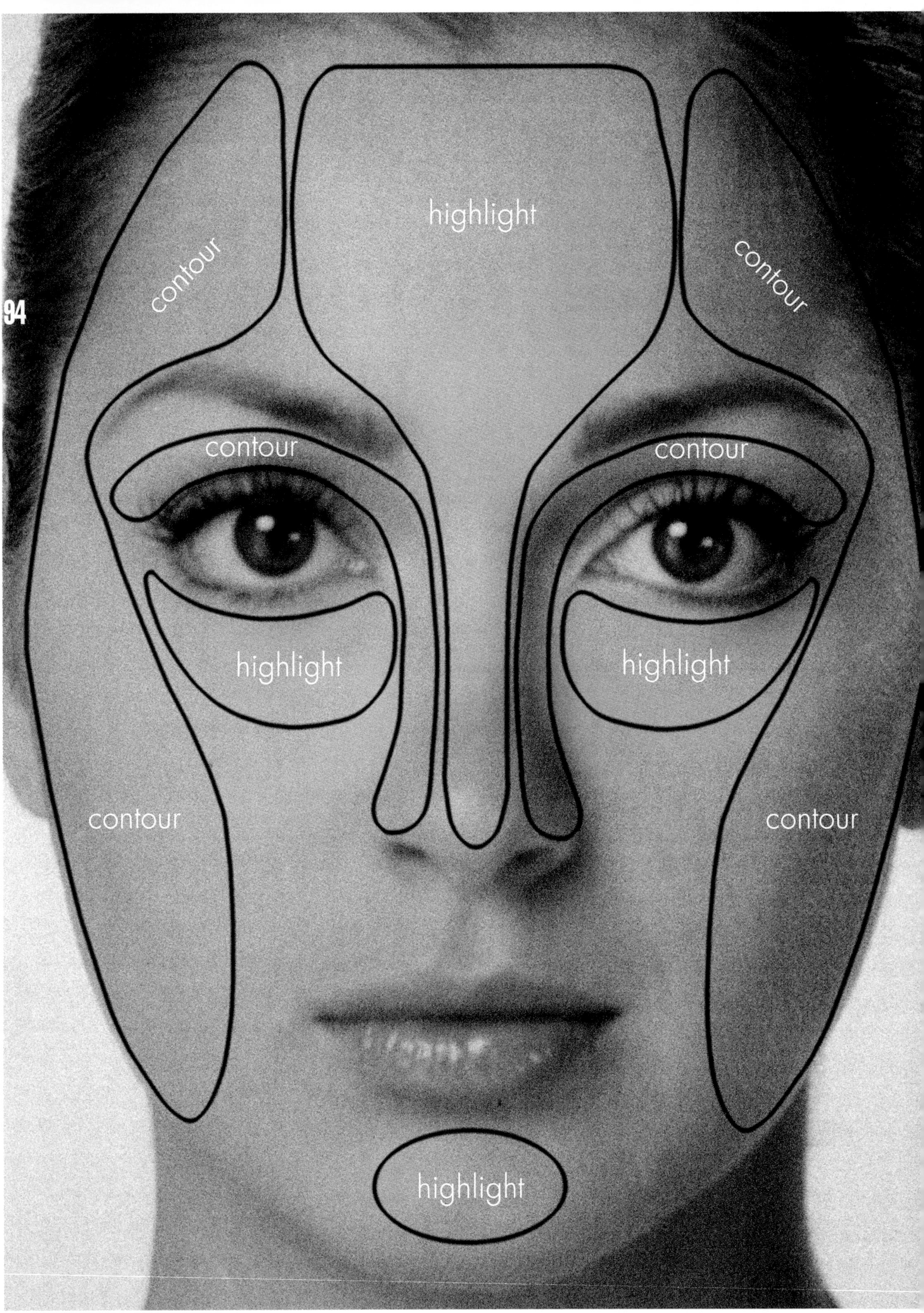

highlight

contour

contour

94

contour

contour

highlight

highlight

contour

contour

highlight

SCULPTING THE FACE

Many women feel they have a full face they'd like to make look slimmer.

The best and most effective way to achieve this is to sculpt the face with foundation and powder. These tools can help give any face shape a more oval appearance.

No matter which product you choose, you will follow the same basic method of application.

You will need at least two contrasting shades. I personally feel that three shades are better.

The first, which will be your base tone, should exactly match your skin's depth of color.

The second, which is your highlight color, should be a shade lighter than your skin.

The third, which is your contour color, should be a shade darker than your skin-tone.

The diagram provided will help you understand the purpose and placement of the three shades.

Please be sure to blend the three shades really well because it is the blending that makes the effect work.

Using foundation, apply your base color first all over your face. Then apply your lightest color to the highlight areas, which are actually those areas of the face you want to "bring out", or in other words, bring into focus.

Lastly, apply your darkest shade to the areas of your face you want to contour, minimize or make appear to recede--such as cheeks that may seem too full, the temples of a wide forehead or the sides of a broad nose.

If you really want to emphasize the effect, follow the basic foundation application with three shades of powder. Doing so will give you a beautifully sculpted three-dimensional effect that should help make any face shape appear more oval.

Tip: Always remember to finish with a light dusting of powder to set your foundation.

tiffany mullen

missy brumley

SKIN LEVEL: 2 (fair)
FACE SHAPE: round-shaped face
EYE SHAPE: droopy eyes
SHADOWS: Highlight-shimmer flesh
Midtone-matte taupe
Contour-shimmer golden brown

OBJECTIVE: to create the illusion of a more oval-shaped face. To make the outer corners of the eye appear to turn up rather than down.

APPLICATION: softly sculpted the cheeks, jaw and temples to create a more oval-shaped face. Made sure to begin all midtone and contour shadow application in slightly from the outside corner of the eyes, making sure to blend up and in to bring attention to the center of the eyelids.

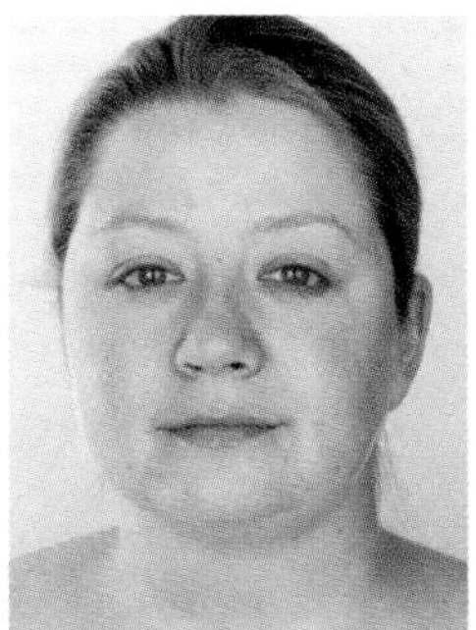

nicki hirt

SKIN LEVEL: 4 (medium)
FACE SHAPE: pear-shaped face

SHADOWS: Highlight- shimmer flesh
Midtone-matte taupe
Contour-shimmer golden brown

OBJECTIVE: to give the illusion of a more oval-shaped face.

APPLICATION: contoured jawline and cheeks to help minimize their width. Highlighted the center of the forehead to create the illusion of more width. Highlighted eyelids and brow bones to open the eyes. Defined the crease and lashline.

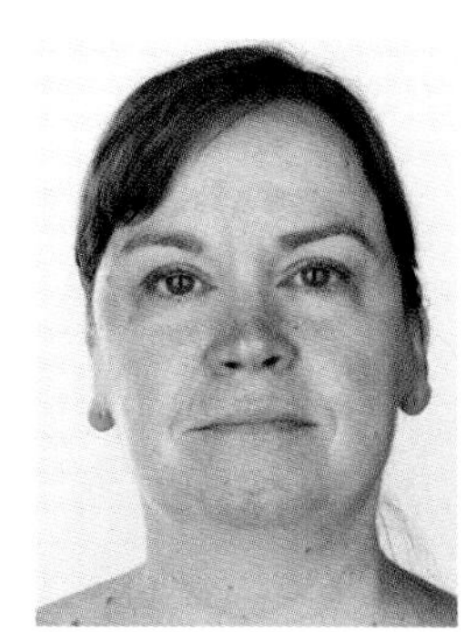

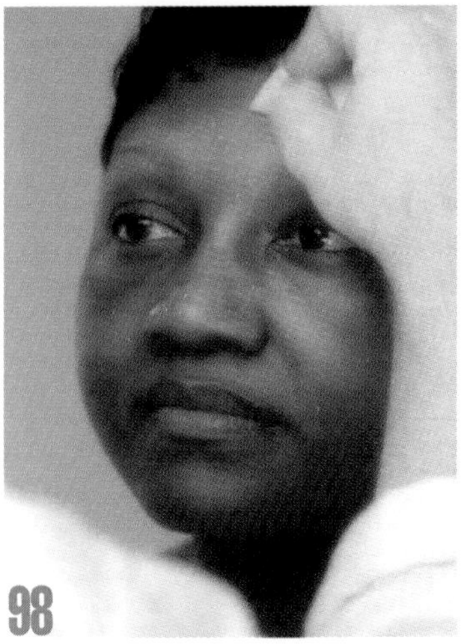

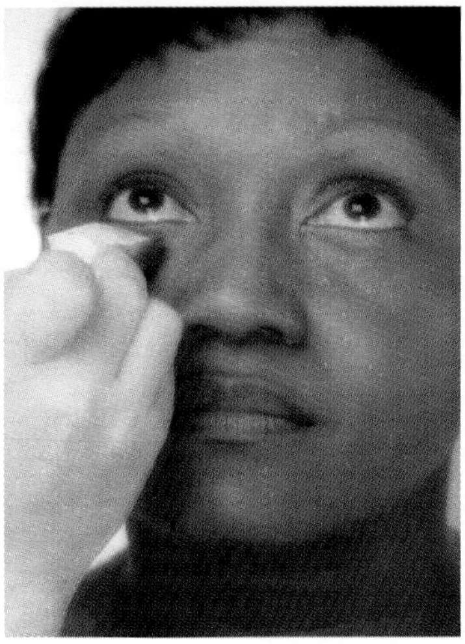

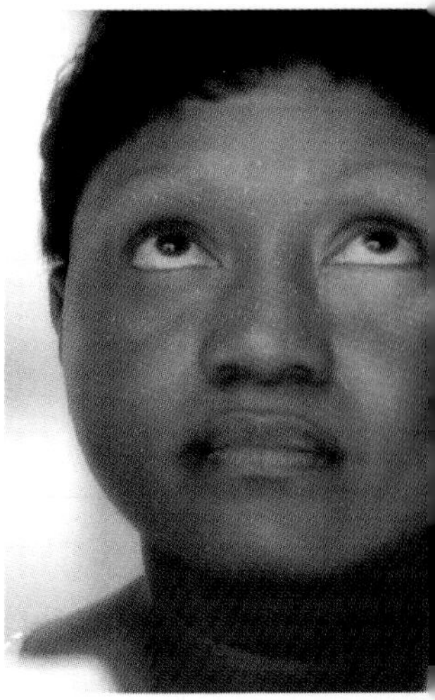

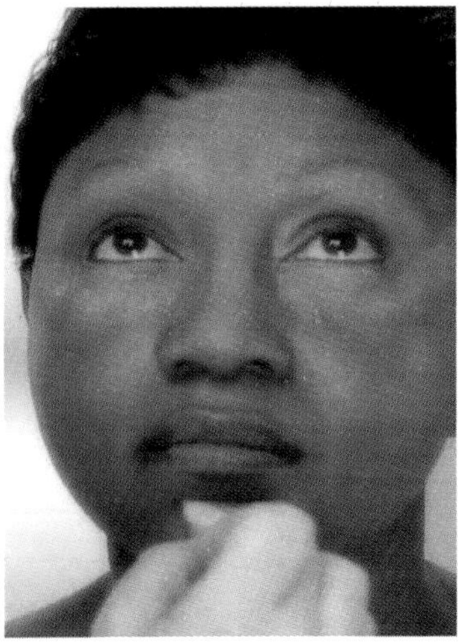

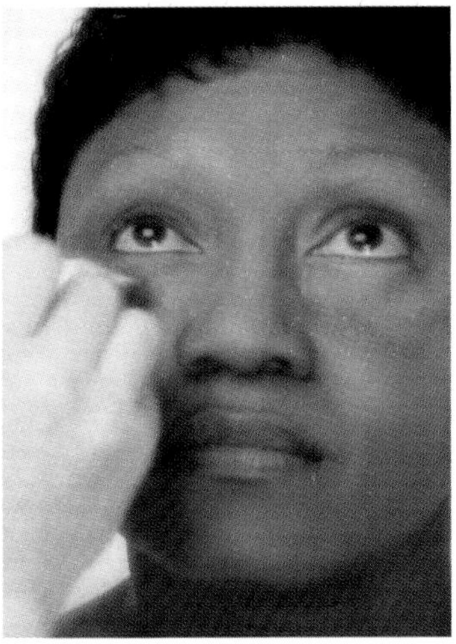

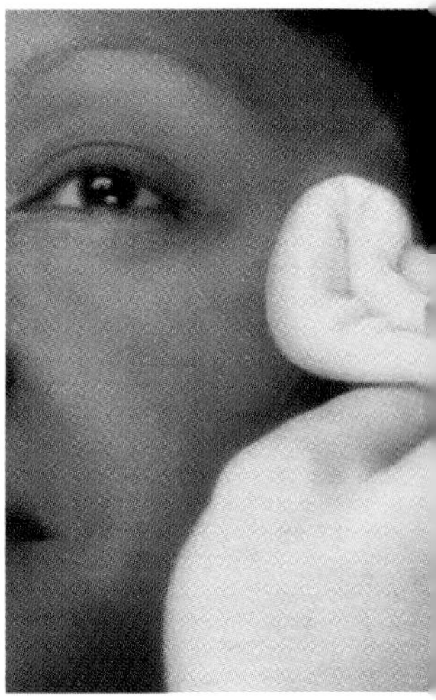

facialmasking

The important thing to remember when improving facial masking is that your goal is to make your skin appear to be one even shade. As I stated earlier, you will need at least two shades of foundation: one to brighten and one to deepen.

The brighter shade is used to help "bring up" the darkest areas to a lighter depth. For medium to light ebony skin, this will usually be a bright golden orange shade. For darker ebony skin, it will usually be a nice, bright, warm brown shade. The warm tone of this shade is so important because it helps to brighten the darker pigments.

Simply apply your brightening shade to all dark, masked areas. Then you will use a shade slightly darker than the brighter areas of your face to deepen those areas that are lighter than the masked area. Apply it to the appropriate areas, being sure to blend the two shades together really well. Follow with the two shades of loose powder that match both shades of your foundation.

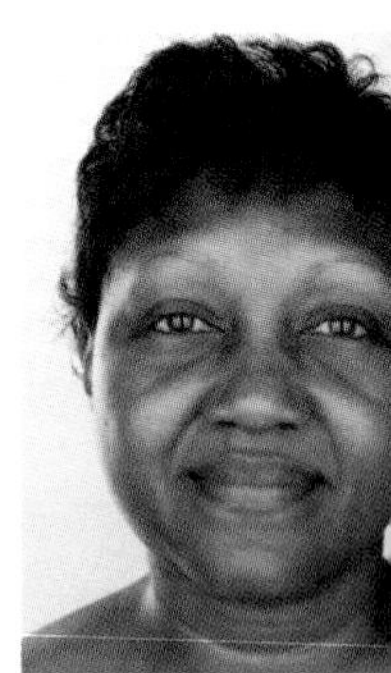

phyllis r. sammons

gloria mayfield-banks

SKIN LEVEL: 12 (light ebony)
FACE SHAPE: oval-shaped face
EYE SHAPE: droopy eyes
SHADOWS: Highlight-shimmer gold
Midtone-matte mahogany
Contour-dark burgandy

OBJECTIVE: to even out skin tone and brighten areas to help add life to the skin. To make the outer corners of the eye appear to turn up rather than down.

APPLICATION: to even out the skin tone used multiple shades of foundation, then brightened the skin with a golden-orange face powder on all the highlight areas of the face. Made sure to begin all midtone and contour shadow application in slightly from the outside corner of the eyes, making sure to blend up and in to bring the attention to the center of the eyelid.

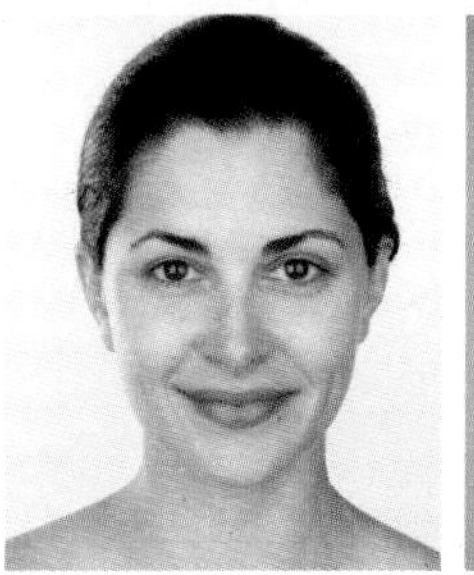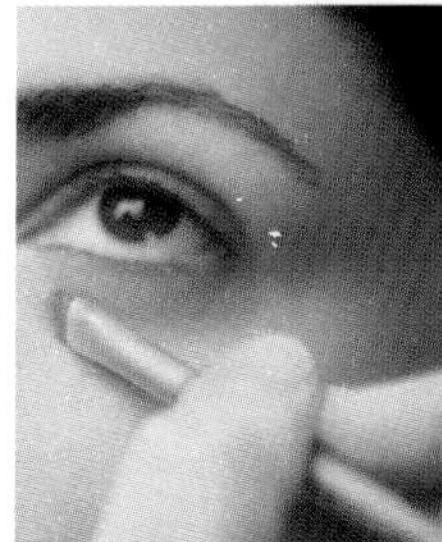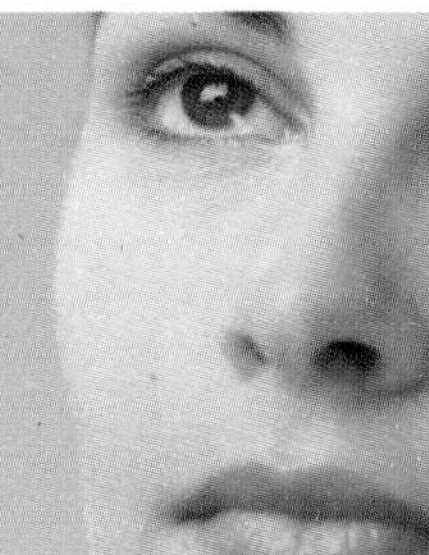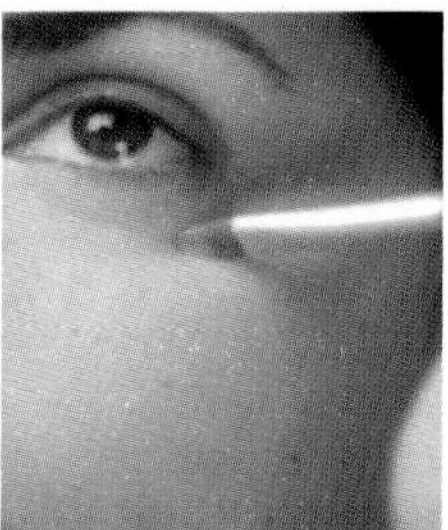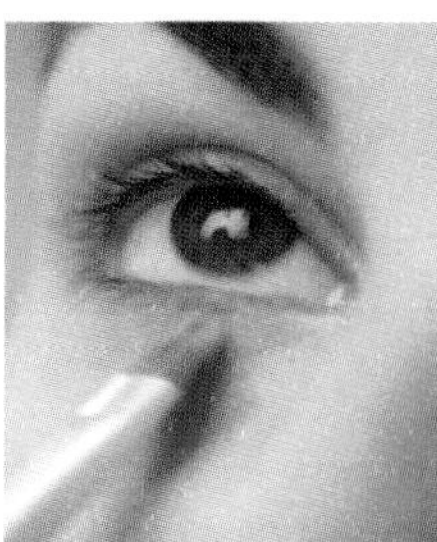

concealer

Concealer can improve your skin's appearance dramatically, but only if it's invisible. The secret to covering under-eye discoloration (which is really blood vessels that appear blue or gray when they reflect light) is choosing the perfect shade and texture. If you use a formula that is too moist it can "travel", slipping into creases and fine lines, drawing attention to what you don't want people to notice. A formula that is too dry is bad for the delicate skin around the eyes and can draw attention to those same flaws. You might need to experiment to find the perfect formula for you. You should choose the same shade as your foundation, or a shade or two lighter if you have truly dark under-eye circles.

If you're using a concealer that matches your foundation exactly you may apply it either before or after your foundation. But if you're using one that is lighter, it is best to apply it first.

darkcircles

First prepare the eye area by applying eye crème and letting it soak in for two or three minutes. Blot away any excess with a sponge or tissue. Using eye crème will help your concealer adhere, and if the skin under your eyes tends to be dry, your concealer won't end up with an undesirable caked-on appearance.

When covering circles, use a fine-tip brush, a sponge or your fingers to trace your concealer along the lowest part of the circle, taking care not to stray beneath the shadowed area. Work outward from the inner corner of the eye, leaving approximately an eighth-of-an-inch between the concealed area and the lower lashline. If you put it too close to the lashline you chance making your eyes look smaller. Blend by dabbing carefully with your fingertip until it seems to disappear. Don't forget to use a little at the inside corners of your eyes because the skin tends to be darker there.

If you do have serious dark under-eye circles and are using a concealer that is a shade or two lighter than your foundation, I advise you to apply it first then put your foundation over it. Be gentle when you blend or you'll risk removing a major part of it with the foundation.

Tip: If you have mature skin, concealer and heavy powder can settle into under-eye lines and wrinkles. Since you won't want to accentuate them with too much powder, use your fingertip to dab on just the tiniest trace.

rebecca roome

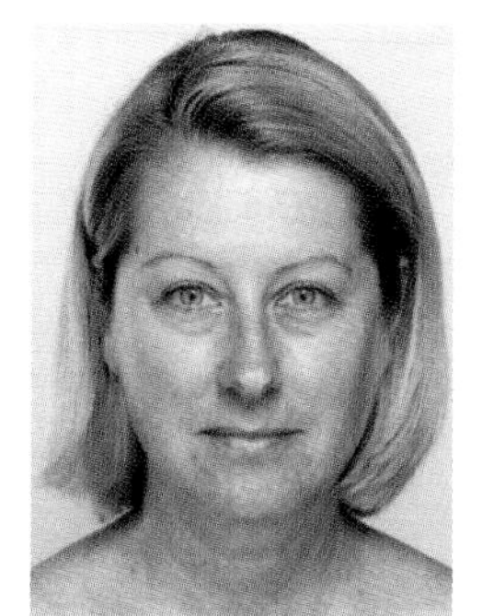

under-eyepuffiness

Unfortunately, and as much as it pains me to say this, the appearance of under-eye bags and puffiness cannot be improved by concealer. The concealer actually draws attention to the puffiness, so it shows up even more. The solution is to highlight underneath the bag to divert attention from it. With a fine-tip brush, simply apply a concealer or a light-reflecting product directly to the shadowed area created by the bag. Adding lightness to this area will counteract its receded appearance and minimize the visual effects of your puffiness.

Tip: Using a concealer that's too light will only draw attention to what you're trying to cover.

Tip: Concealer can be made sheerer by mixing it with a little eye-crème.

Tip: You can test coverage by applying a little concealer to a vein on the inside of your wrist.

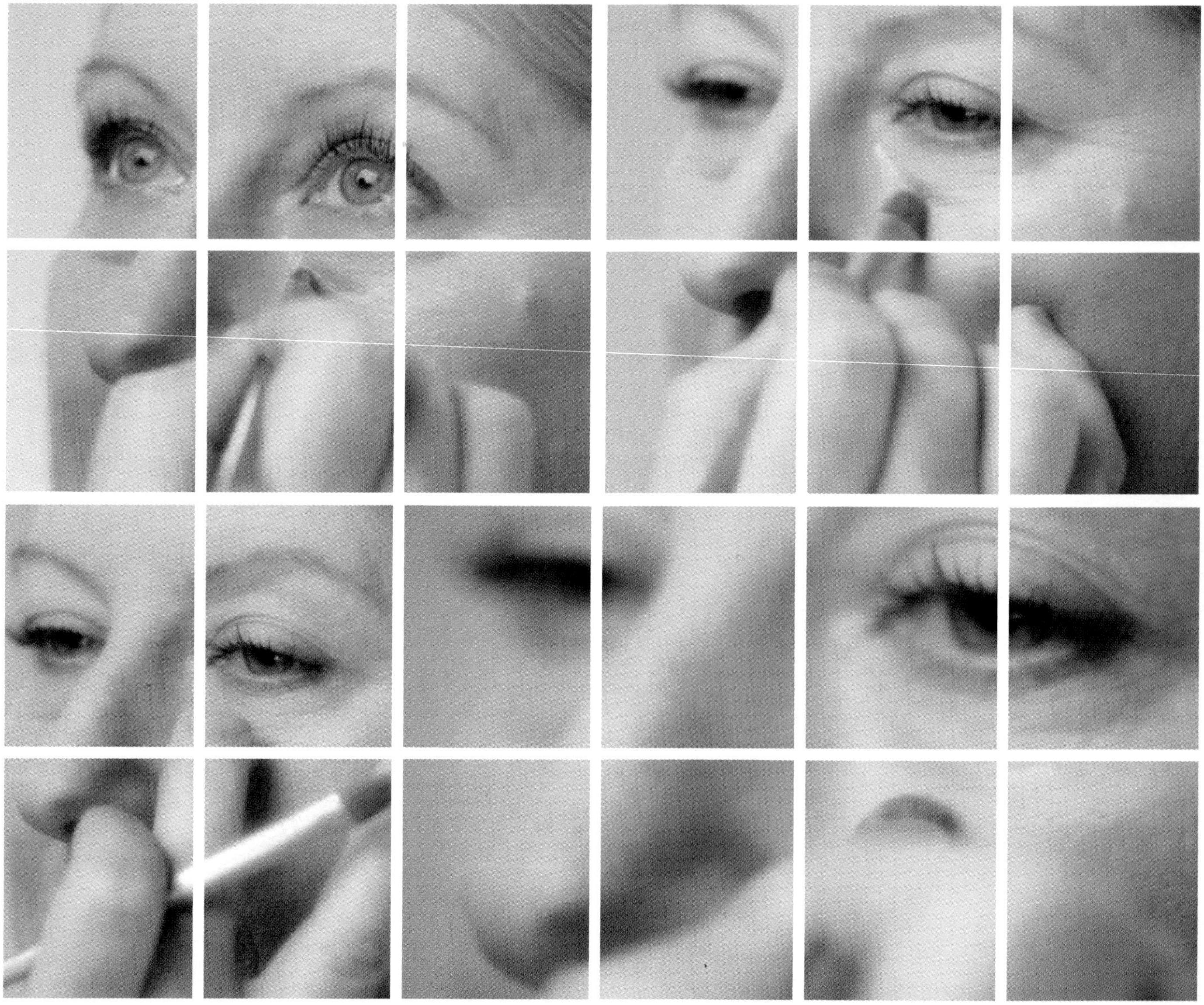

madeleine zeisler

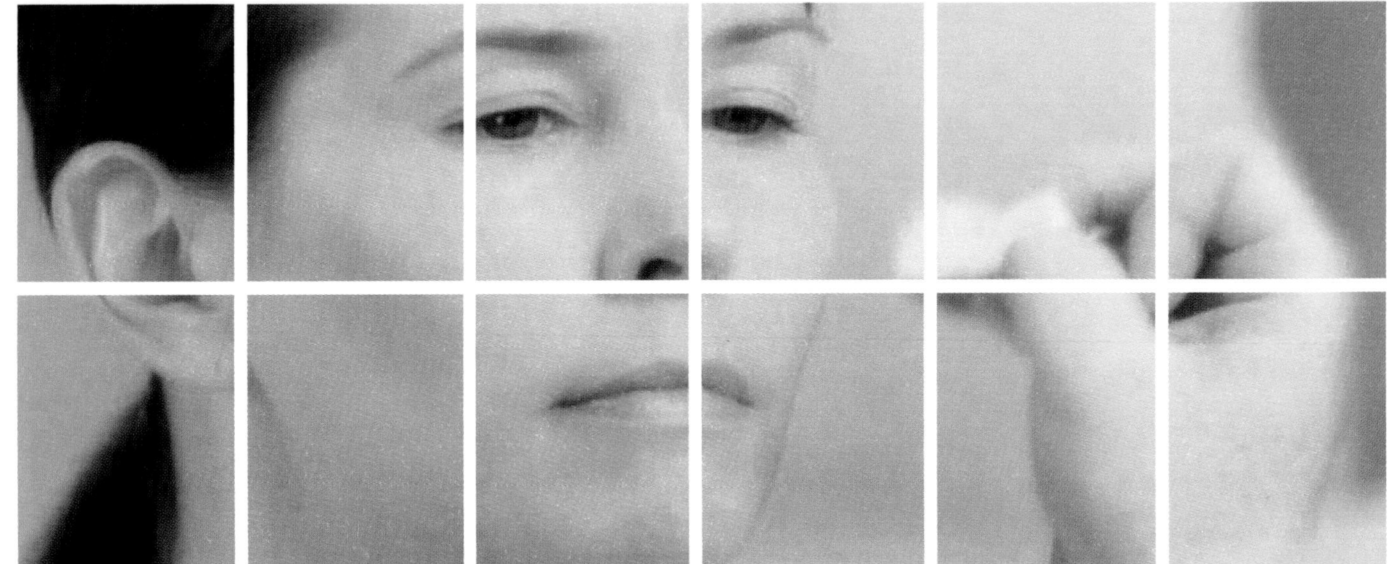

discoloration

Remember that concealers of different textures are used for different problem areas. The texture you use to minimize facial blemishes should be a little drier because it will cling better. These drier-texture concealers are formulated so as not to irritate breakouts. This is the one place you'll want to make sure that your concealer matches exactly because using one that is too light will only draw attention to raised blemishes.

A brush works well for applying concealer directly onto those harder to cover blemishes. Don't forget to gently dab with your fingertip to blend and smooth the outer edges. A longer-wearing, drier formula applied with a fine-tip brush will also work well for concealing broken capillaries, but you can also trace them with a pencil concealer then gently blend. Pencil concealers work well here because you simply draw them on.

When covering rosacea or hyper-pigmentation, first use a brush to apply your concealer directly to the discolored area, then gently dab the outer edges with your finger to blend it.

scars

Scar tissue is smooth and harder for the concealer to grab, so you should use a heavier, drier one such as a solid-crème-stick or pot because it will stay on better. Simply apply it to the scarred area with a brush then blend the outer edges. Always remember to powder over your concealer to prevent it from "traveling". But be careful because concealer does grab powder differently than foundation due to its high level of pigment.

Tip: Yellow-based shades look healthier and more natural.

Tip: Using corrective green, pink or violet concealers will only turn your face colors.

Tip: To get that perfect shade of concealer, try mixing it with a little of your foundation.

karie roberti

SKIN LEVEL: 4 (medium)
FACE SHAPE: square-shaped face
EYE SHAPE: hooded eyes
SHADOWS: Highlight-shimmer beige
Midtone-matte taupe
Contour-dark matte taupe
OBJECTIVE: to give the illusion of a more oval-shaped face. To minimize the hooded appearance of the eyelids,making her eyes appear more open.
APPLICATION: contoured hairline and jawline to soften the "four corners". Highlighted down the center of the forehead, nose and chin. Using midtone colors, applied and layered on the hooded area, giving the illusion that the area recedes.

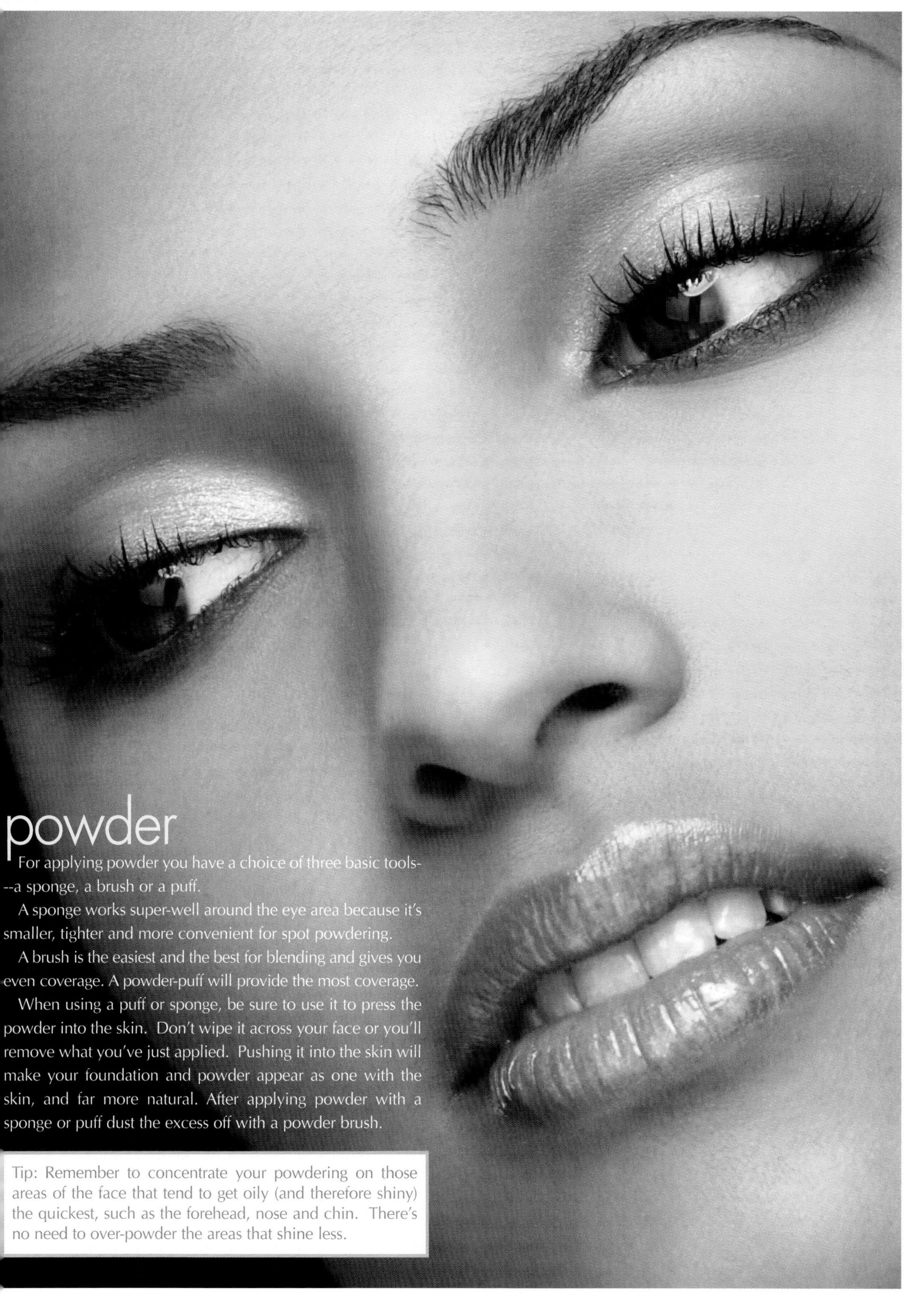

powder

For applying powder you have a choice of three basic tools--a sponge, a brush or a puff.

A sponge works super-well around the eye area because it's smaller, tighter and more convenient for spot powdering.

A brush is the easiest and the best for blending and gives you even coverage. A powder-puff will provide the most coverage.

When using a puff or sponge, be sure to use it to press the powder into the skin. Don't wipe it across your face or you'll remove what you've just applied. Pushing it into the skin will make your foundation and powder appear as one with the skin, and far more natural. After applying powder with a sponge or puff dust the excess off with a powder brush.

Tip: Remember to concentrate your powdering on those areas of the face that tend to get oily (and therefore shiny) the quickest, such as the forehead, nose and chin. There's no need to over-powder the areas that shine less.

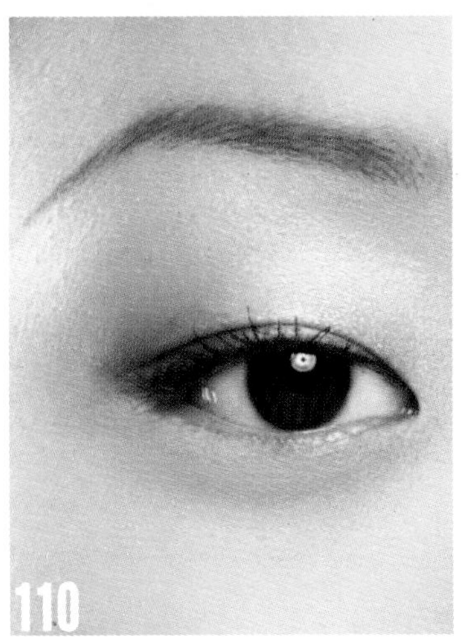

Before we begin to apply color it is important to examine and define e shapes. Perhaps you feel you don't have the optimal eye shape. May you think they are too small, too close set, or just not perfect. No matt how you feel, this information about eye shapes will help you to optimi what God gave you.

susan freeman

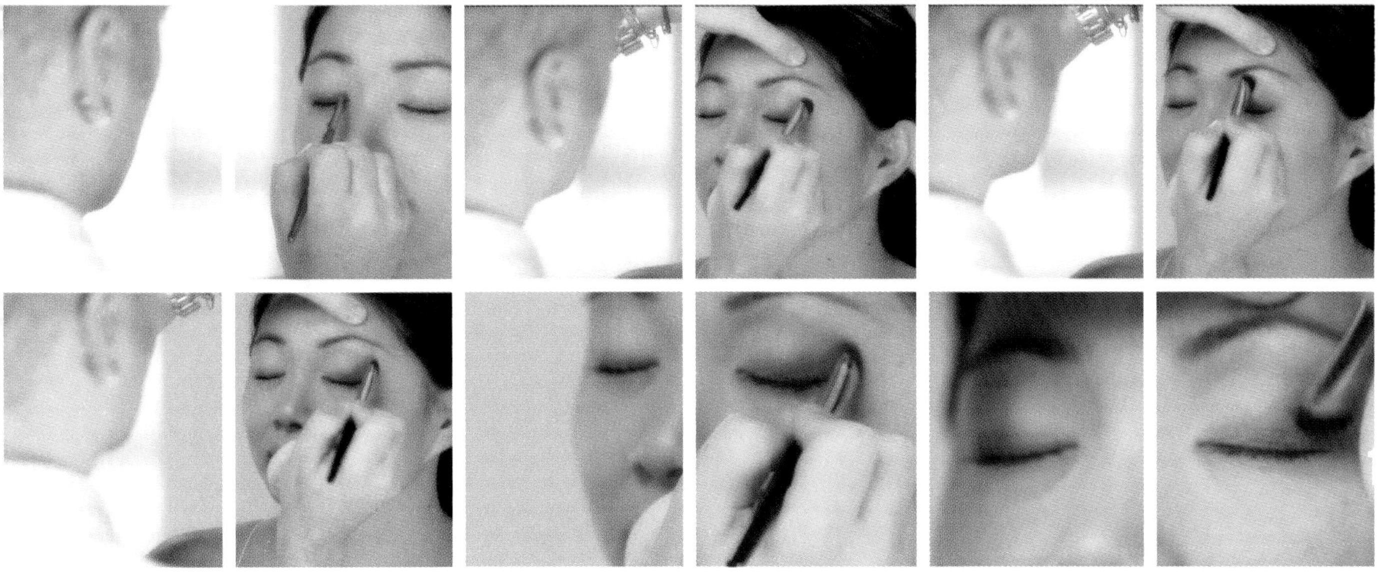

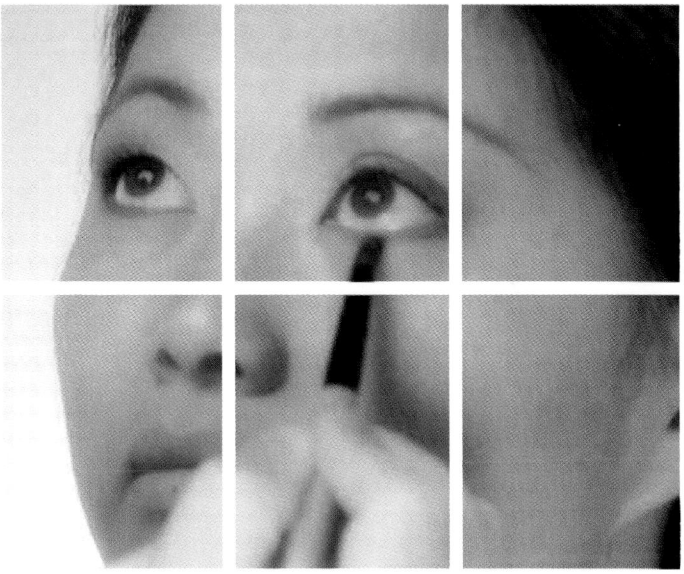

hoodedeyes

Hooded eyes are sometimes referred to as bedroom eyes because the lids tend to look partly closed. Your goal is to make your eye appear more open by minimizing the lid.

**Never use a really dark shadow over the entire lid because it makes it appear heavier and therefore more closed rather than open.

**Highlight the inner portion of your eyelid.

**Starting at your lashline, blend and contour upward using a medium tone shadow. Medium-tone defining-shadow works better than a really dark tone because it will help the lid recede and won't appear too harsh. You can always layer it if you want more depth, plus it's easier to blend than one that's too dark.

**You can define your lashline, just make sure that your line is thick enough to show with your eyes open.

**Don't be tempted to highlight your brow bone too much because doing so can accentuate the hooded appearance of the eyelid.

> Tip: The eyebrow shape is very important here because attention can be diverted from the hooded eyelid with a beautifully done eyebrow.

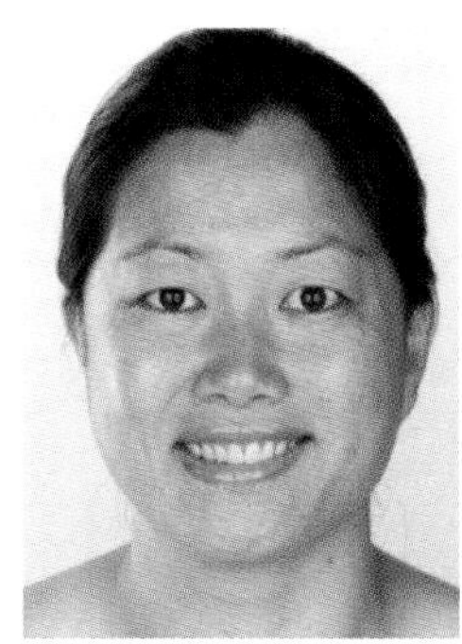

pam shaw

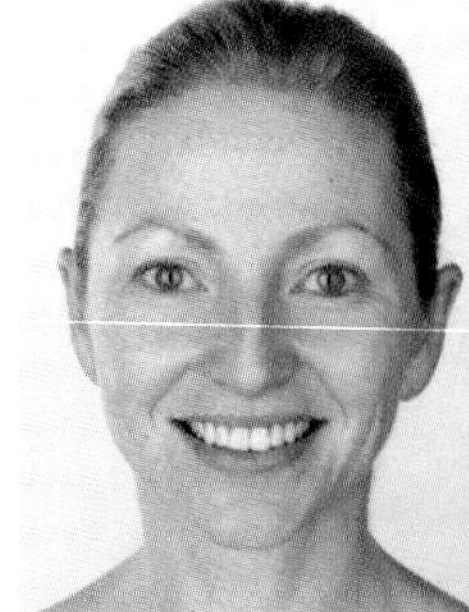

wide-seteyes

If the spacing between your eyes is wider than the width of one eye, your eyes are considered wide-set. Your goal is to create the illusion that they are set closer together.

**This is one instance when you can use a slightly darker mid-tone shadow on the inside hollow of your eye, next to the bridge of your nose. This will help the area appear to recede and make your eyes seem closer together.

**Begin all dark color application slightly in from the outer corners, and always blend your shadow in and up instead of outward because that will "pull" the eyes out, and we are trying to pull them in.

**Eyeliner may be used on the lashline but should not extend beyond the outer edge of the eye because doing so will only negate all your efforts to make your eyes appear closer.

jan harris

smalleyes

Some of you probably feel that you have small eyes. There are certainly things you can do to help them appear larger.

**Avoid really dark shadows on the lid because it tends to close in the eye.

**Highlight your lid to help bring out your eyes and open them up.

**Contour the crease and above to direct focus to your eyes.

**Define around your eyes right at the lashline to bring them out.

**Well-defined, curled, plumped lashes work really well to open up small eyes.

> Tip: To open them up, and give the illusion of appearing larger you can apply white or beige eyeliner around the inside "wet tissue" of the eyes.

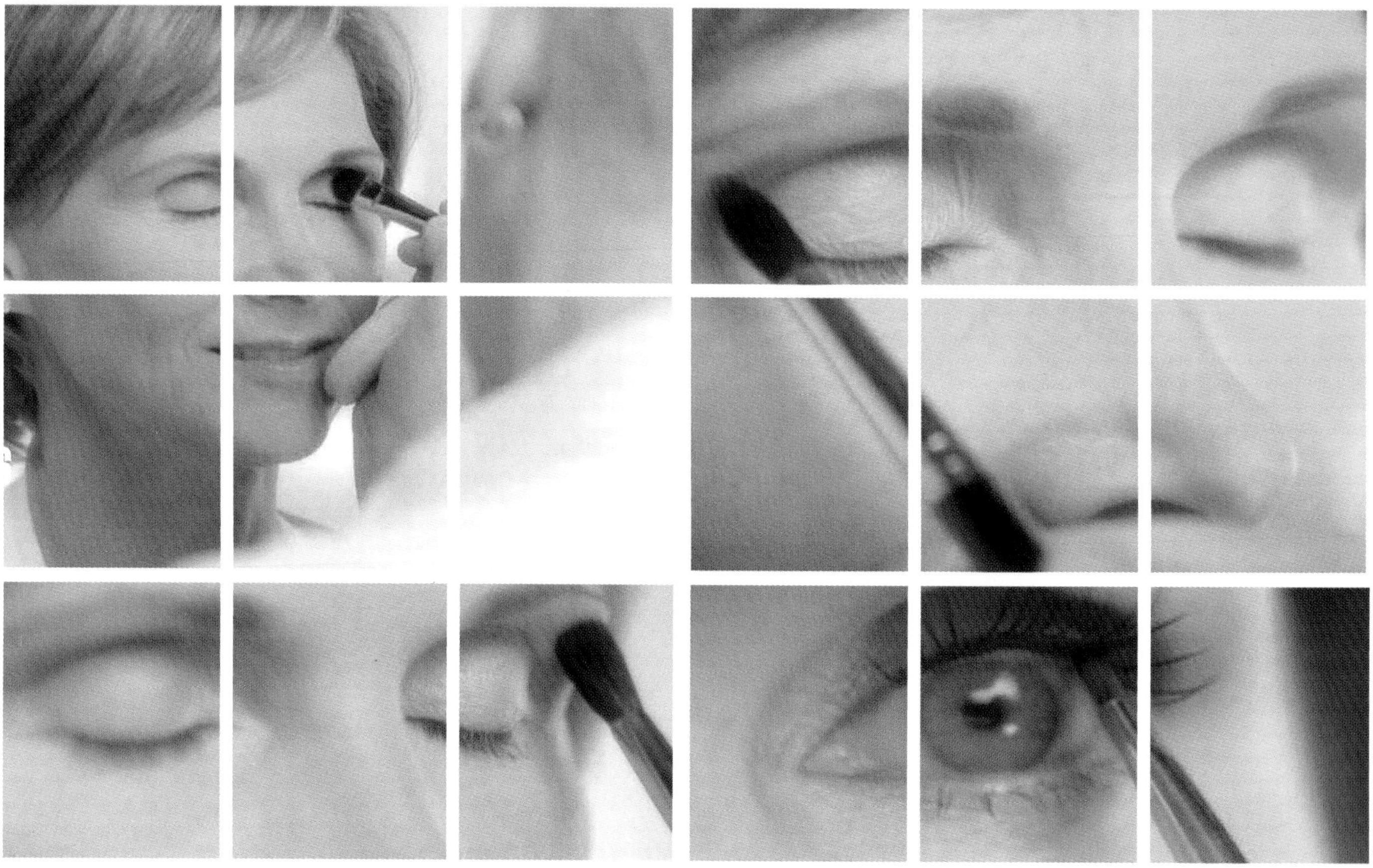

deep-seteyes

Deep-set eyes are eyes that are set deep in their sockets.

If you have deep-set eyes you are lucky because you already have God-given eye shadow. The goal with deep-set eyes is to bring them out and make them more noticeable. They can tend to appear small if you're not careful when applying your shadow.

**Use a light to medium shadow---usually one with shimmer---on the lid itself to expand its appearance and "bring it out" toward you.

**Avoid putting the contour actually in the crease. Instead, place the contour---a medium tone, not too dark---a little above the crease to minimize your brow-bone.

**Don't overly highlight the brow-bone itself because with deep-set eyes it's already prominent.

**Line your eyes at lashline to help define them. The line should be very fine closest to the nose, becoming wider toward the outer edge of the eye.

Tip: Never do a dark lid because it can close in your eye and make it appear smaller.

Tip: For drama I always use a brighter (not necessarily a darker) color of shadow.

judie mccoy

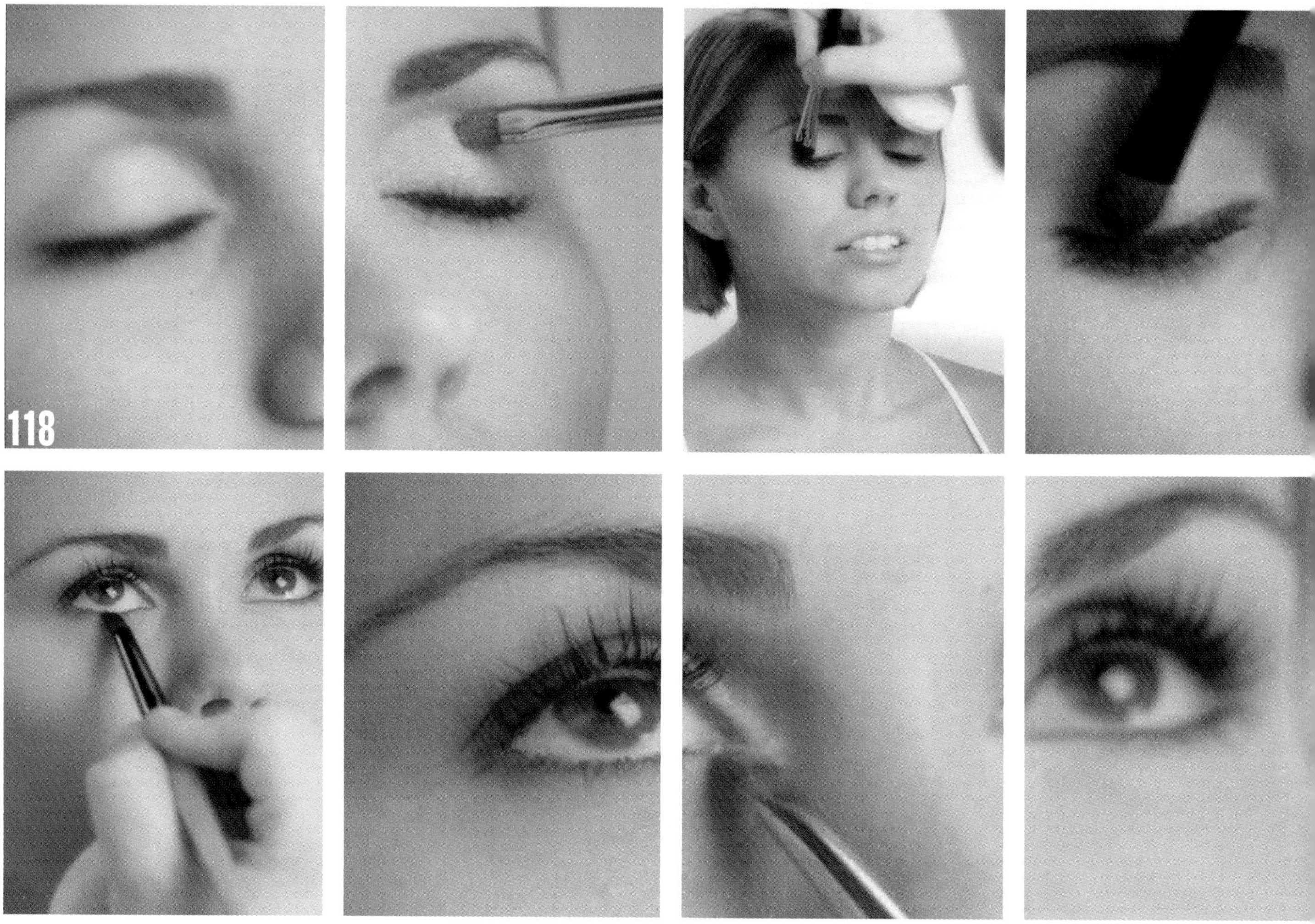

close-seteyes

The average spacing between a pair of eyes is approximately the width of one eye. If your eyes are spaced any closer, you are considered to have close-set eyes. Your goal is to create the illusion of them being wider apart.

**Keep the inner corners light and bright by using a light-color, shimmer, highlighting-shadow. It will "open up" your eyes and give the illusion of more space between them.

**Shade and define the outer corners with your deepest tone. It will help "pull your eyes apart" and balance your face.

taylor moore

lisa madson

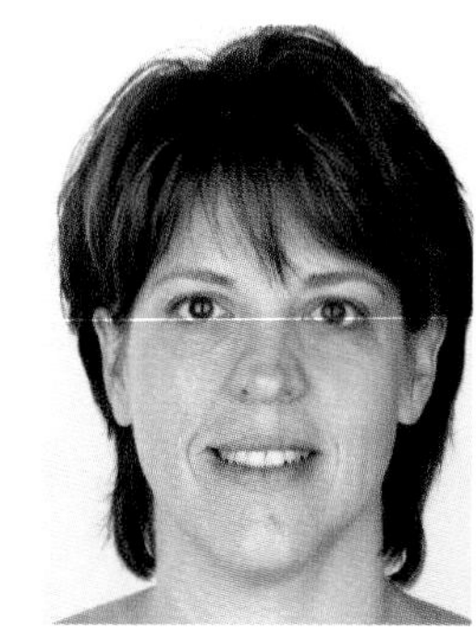

droopyeyes

Droopy eyes slope downward at the outer corners. They are sometimes referred to as "sad puppy eyes". Your goal is to make the outer corners appear as if they turn up rather than down.

**Use eyeliner sparingly since it can draw attention to the way your eyes turn down at the outer corners, especially on the bottom, where the use of eyeliner tends to "pull them down" even more.

**Apply your shadow color slightly in from the outermost corner of the eye and extend it up, keeping the focus of attention more toward the center of the eyelid.

**Definitely highlight the brow bone to draw attention up, rather than down.

**Start the mascara on the lashes a little bit in from the outer corners. Concentrate the mascara more heavily on the lashes at the center of the eye and the inside corners to divert attention away from the outer corners.

**Eyebrows should curve outward, gently---most definitely not in an exaggerated downward arch.

> Tip: If you do want to wear color at your lower lashline begin your application about an eighth-of-an-inch in from the outermost corner.

10 basic application

Now we are at the fun part---applying color. In this chapter we will discuss basic color applications. Get out those brushes; it is time to paint.

sunni smyth

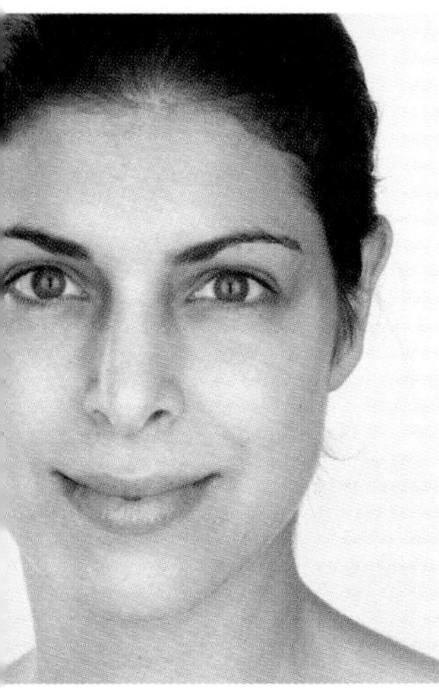
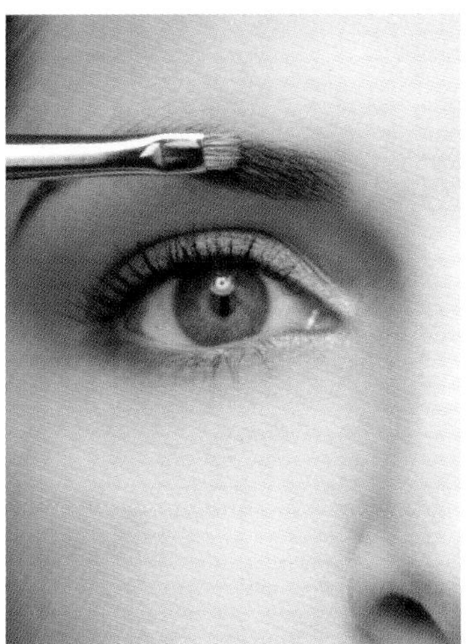

brows

When selecting a brow color choose one that is either your natural color or one shade lighter. Be careful not to confuse brow-pencils and powders with eye-pencils and shadows---they are not the same.

Brow-pencils are duller in color, usually with no sheen, and have a little more wax in their texture than do eyeliner pencils. Eyebrow powder is duller and more matte than eye shadow.

When using a brow-pencil, apply short, feathery, hair-like strokes angled in the same direction as the hairs' growth. Never draw on a solid, hard-looking line. Short feather-like strokes are meant to imitate short little hairs. I prefer to go over the area again, using a small angled brush, following the same stroke pattern. It blends it in a little better and helps it appear more natural.

You can also achieve a very natural brow by using brow-powder. Apply it with a small, stiff, angled brush in short, feathery strokes while following the natural hair-growth pattern.

For those with scars or brows that are just not there, you may need the coverage of a crème brow-color. It gives the most coverage. Simply apply it with a stiff, angled brush using short feathery strokes. It's always best to follow crème with a brow-powder to set it and help it last all day.

Whichever method you prefer, when grooming your brows, always finish by using a brow-brush to brush upward and outward. If you like, you can end with a brow-gel. It will act like a hairspray for the brows.

> Tip: Sharpen your pencil each time you use it.

> Tip: You can use eyebrow pencil or eyebrow powder separately, or you can combine them. If you combine them, you'll increase their wearing time.

I think that now might be the best time to discuss the theory of light versus dark. I know most of you have heard it before, but for those who haven't (or maybe you forgot), here goes.

Anytime you use a light color it brings whatever you apply it to toward you. Whatever you darken recedes away from you. This theory is especially important in applying eye shadow because that is where you do most of your shading.

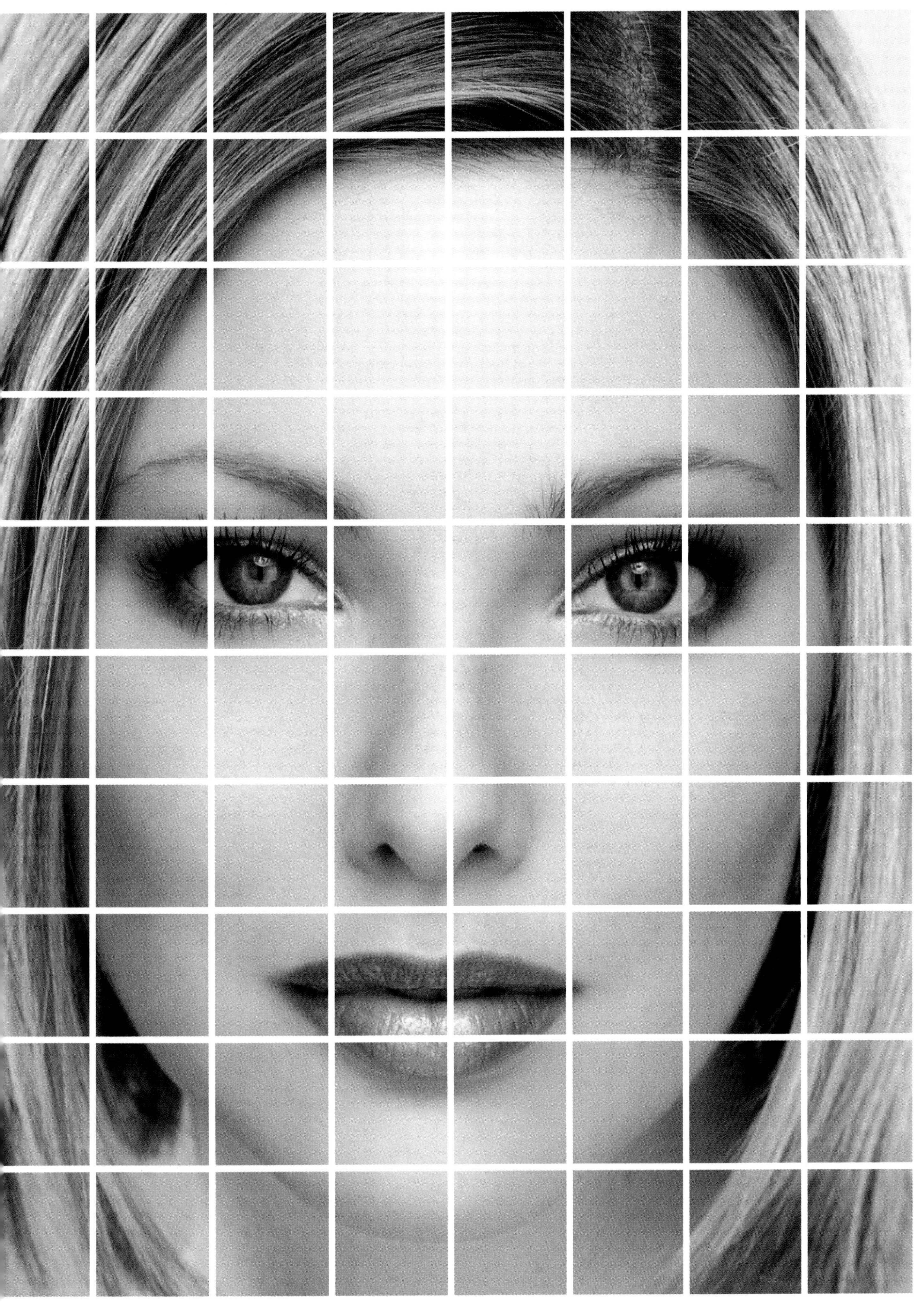

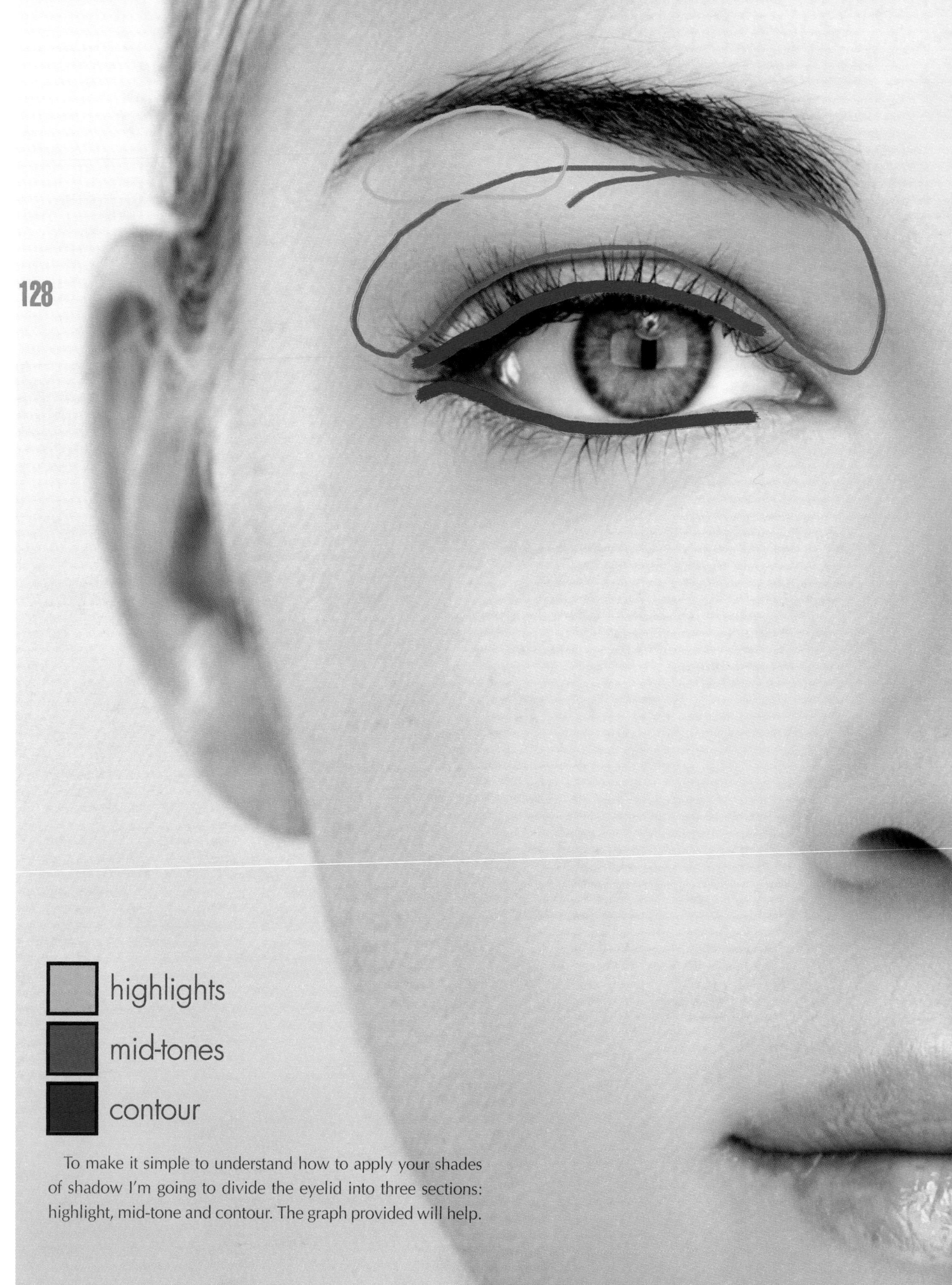

To make it simple to understand how to apply your shades of shadow I'm going to divide the eyelid into three sections: highlight, mid-tone and contour. The graph provided will help.

HIGHLIGHT

Your highlight can be matte or shimmer. I personally prefer it to be shimmer because I think it's more effective and opens the eye up more. I find it especially effective when highlighting the deep-set eye.

The undertone of your highlighter can really change the effect it creates. However, it should always be the proper undertone for your skin. For example, if the undertone is very fleshy, it will be subtle and natural. If it is very pale (almost white or beige), it will create a very dramatic effect.

The finish can also effect the overall look by how much it changes the shape. A matte finish will give you a subtle change. A sheen or shimmer will create a much more dramatic shape change because not only will the depth be changing your eyelid shape, the reflection of the sheen will increase the effect.

For example, you can apply your highlight color to your brow-bone and lid area to help give the eyelid a more three-dimensional shape. You can use it on both areas or either, depending on how much shaping of the lid you want to achieve.

MIDTONE

Selecting the correct mid-tone color is most important because it is the main component in building the eyelid shape and the first step in blending your contour color. Your mid-tone color is usually, though not always, matte.

Bearing in mind the shade of your skin and its undertones is vital when making your color selection because it is an extension of your complexion. I find that using a compatible, neutral, natural shade works best, and it can be layered for depth of color.

> Tip: You could also use a blush for your mid-tone if the product has been approved for the eye. It's very important to remember that mid-tone color begins your blending process.

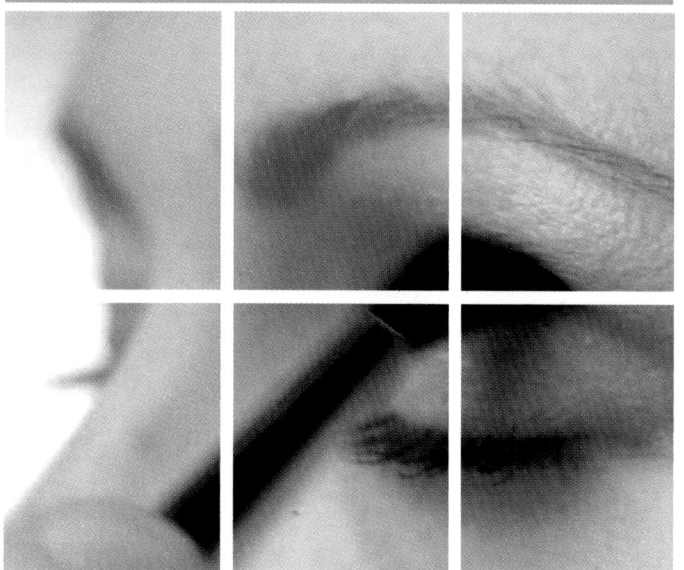

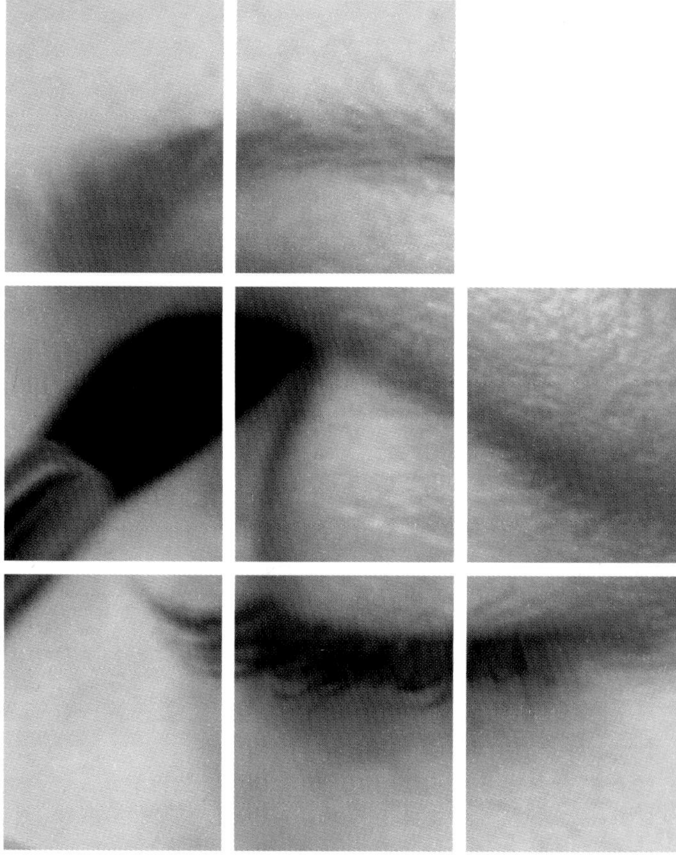

First, start to apply the mid-tone shadow by brushing it in the crease starting from the outside, working in and up toward the brow on the inside plane of the eyelid. This begins the eyelid shape.

Next, if you don't have a very defined crease, this is where you begin the process of creating one. Using a fine-tipped brush, start by applying another layer where you want to deepen your crease, then blend. If you like, you may apply multiple layers or a slightly darker color for additional depth of color, but always remember to blend, blend and blend!

If you like, your mid-tone may be used alone---just swept across the eyelid for a very natural look. The mid-tone color can also be used from lashline to brow. It's a very simple look that can make the eye color pop, but it won't help to create lid shape, and it does tend to "flatten" the eyelids.

> Tip: A quick note: the first place you lay your brush will receive the most color because it has the most product on it at this time.

> Tip: Since blending is so vital to the overall effect of beautifully painted eyes, good quality shadow-brushes are a must because they enable you to create artful shapes and effects.

> Tip: You should apply your concealer or foundation then your powder onto your lids before you begin with the eye shadow because it helps the shadow blend more easily and wear longer.

CONTOUR

Just because it defines the eye does not mean that your contour color must be stark or dark, though it will always be the deepest of your shades. This is where you will most often use color, especially deep metallic shadows. You'll find that most makeup lines have more contour colors because they are the most fun and exciting to use.

It can be either matte or shimmer and is usually applied at the lashline and worked up into the crease.

Start by taking a brush with shadow and blending it across your top lashline from the outside corner, inward. Next, apply color up into the crease, starting at the outer corner and blending inward. By continuing to apply your contour color into the crease on top of your mid-tone, the depth of the color will deepen the crease.

If you want a more dramatic eye, you can use your contour color over the entire lid beginning at the lashline then blending upward.

When using your contour color over the entire lid, I can't impress upon you enough that in this particular instance you have to blend, blend and blend because with this type of eye the entire look is in the blending.

> Tip: Contour in a medium-depth color that's layered for added intensity also works very well.

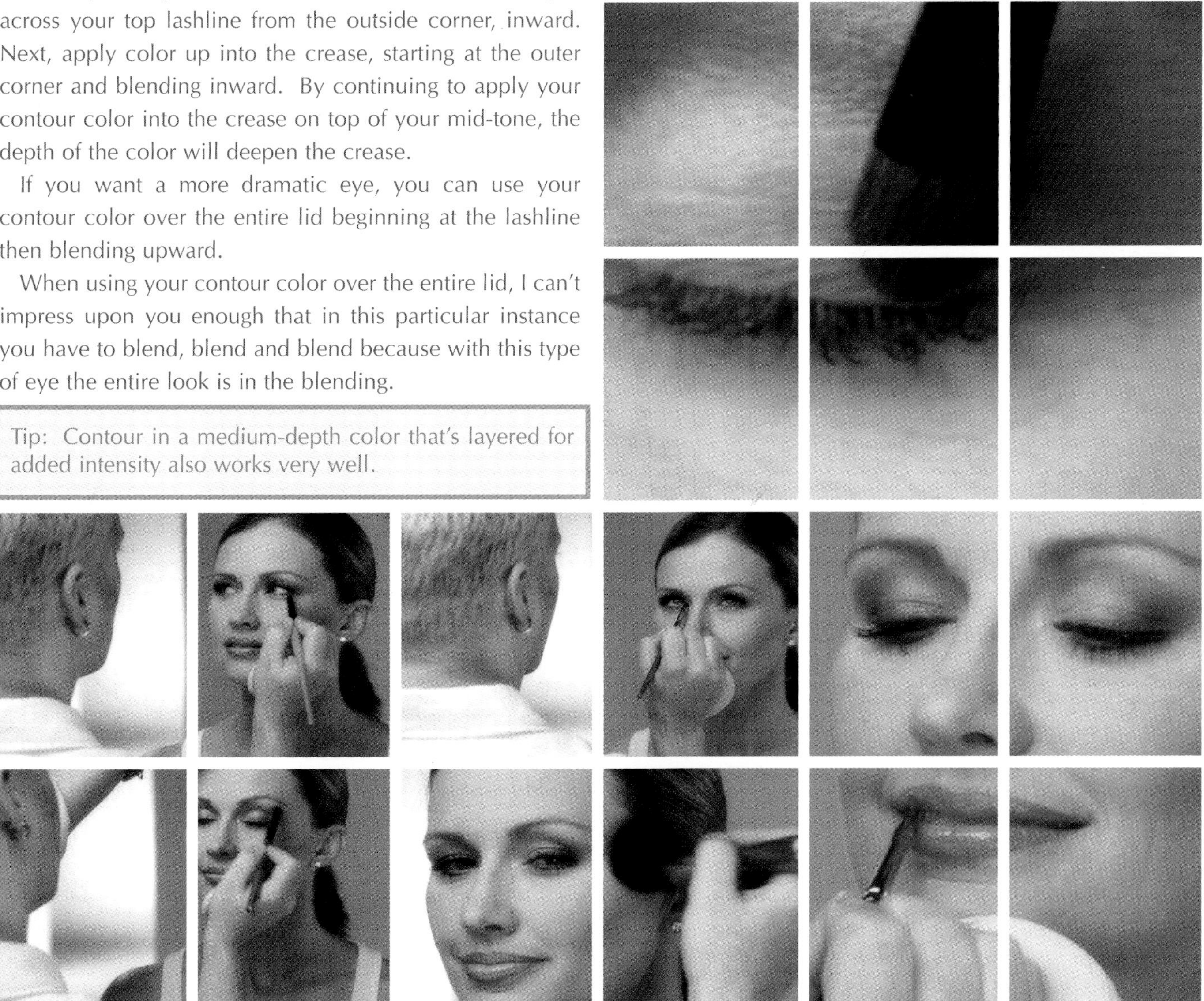

EYELINER

You can use pencil, liquid, cake, creme or powder for this step---or skip it completely.

Many PENCILS these days contain silicone. The silicone enables them to glide on nicely and makes them easy to blend.

When using a pencil, begin at the outside corner, draw small, feather-like strokes, connecting each one as you move toward the inside of the eye, then blend with a small brush. Using that same brush, apply a powder-shadow to help set your pencil and make it look more natural. It will also help correct any mistakes you might have made by blending everything together.

Unless you want to achieve a highly dramatic look for evening, I'd advise you to define under the eye with shadow rather than pencil. Shadow gives a softer, more natural look. I personally think that you should never use a pencil under the eyes because it appears harsh, but if you do, always follow by brushing on powder-shadow to help blend the line.

My own favorite method is to use a small brush to push black powder up into the lashes at the root line. It defines the eye without making it appear lined, and it makes the lashes look really thick.

On some women a tiny rim of skin might still be visible between the lashes and the eye, so to ensure optimal shaping it's best to darken it with a powder otherwise the eye will not pop as effectively. You could also use a soft pencil that smudges.

LIQUID eyeliner is the longest wearing, and most brands are available with a fine brush. Liquid creates the strongest, most dramatic line. Never use liquid under the eye because the result appears too stark and hard.

When using liquid eyeliner, draw in a continuous line starting at the inside corner of the eye to the outside corner of the eye, giving the line a little "kick up" at the end. Liquid eyeliner is the most difficult to use, but you can master it with a little practice.

CAKE eyeliner comes in a creamy, powder form. It is applied with a small damp brush using the same method as the liquid eyeliner.

CRÈME eyeliner is also applied with a small damp brush in exactly the same manner as the liquid and the cake.

POWDER eyeliner gives the most natural look and is the easiest to work with. You can use it dry---or wet if you want a stronger look.

To apply it dry, use a brush and beginning at the outside corner of the eye, draw on fine, feathery strokes at the base of the lashes. Continue all the way to the inside corner, connecting the brush strokes.

If you choose to use the powder wet, dampen your brush and apply it just like your liquid eyeliner. It will give you the same effect as liquid, but it is much easier to control.

> Tip: Always keep your pencils sharpened for more precise application.

pam skaggs

roshawnda r. foster

SKIN LEVEL: 11(bronze)
FACE SHAPE: heart-shaped face

SHADOWS: Highlight-shimmer gold
Midtone-matte mahogany
Contour-dark burgundy
OBJECTIVE: to give the illusion of a more oval-shaped face.
APPLICATION: contoured the temples and defined the hollows of the cheeks. This helped minimize the width of those areas. Highlighted the chin to create the illusion of width. Highlighted the lid and brow bone to open the eye. Used the midtone shadow to even out her lids, then defined the lashline really well.

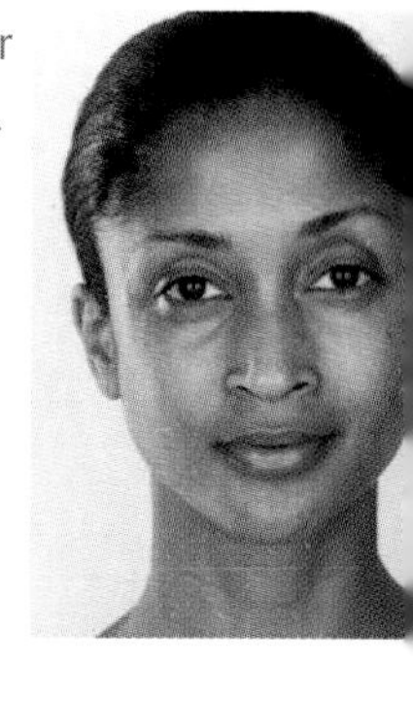

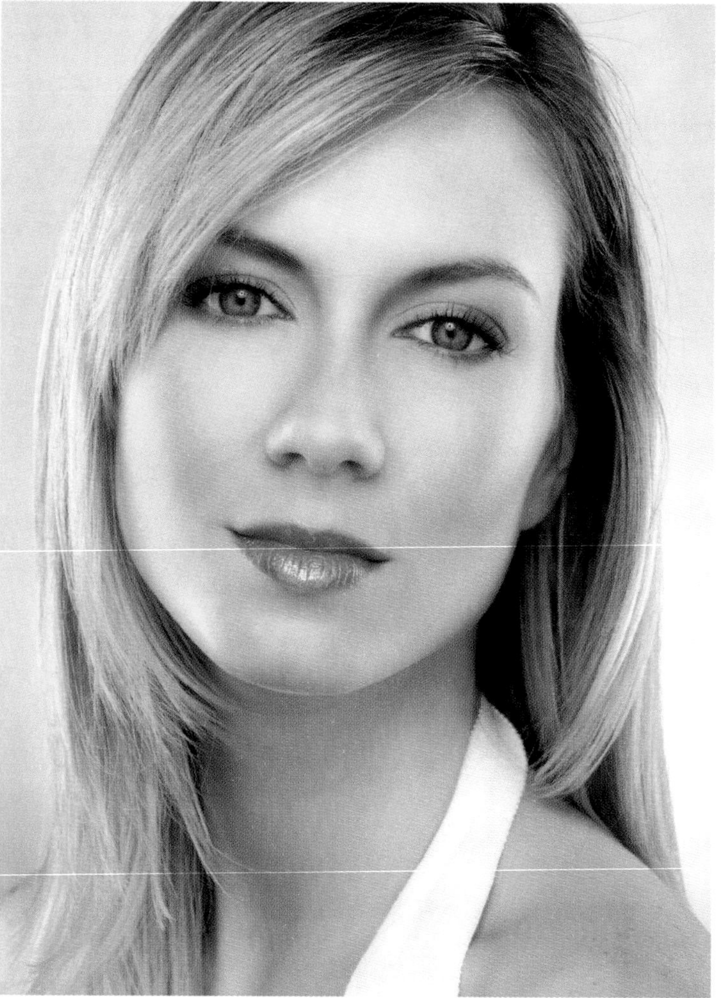

amy mueller

SKIN LEVEL: 4 (medium)
FACE SHAPE: square-shaped face
EYE SHAPE: close-set eyes
SHADOWS: Highlight-shimmer beige
Midtone-matte taupe
Contour-shimmer dark brown
OBJECTIVE: to create the illusion of a more oval-shaped face. To visually pull the eyes apart.
APPLICATION: contoured the hairline and jaw to soften the "four corners". Highlighted down the center of the forehead, nose and tip of the chin. Highlighted the inner corners of the eyelid to visually push the eyes apart. Defined the outer corners of eye with the deepest shadow.

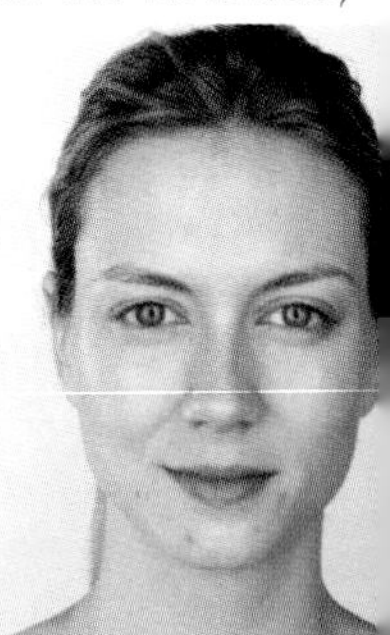

carol monteverde

poppi monroe

mary diamond

SKIN LEVEL: 4 (medium)
FACE SHAPE: round-shaped face
EYE SHAPE: hooded eye
SHADOWS: Highlight-shimmer flesh
Midtone-matte taupe/ matte dark taupe
Contour-shimmer golden brown

OBJECTIVE: to give the illusion of a more oval-shaped face. To minimize the hooded area and "open up" the eye.

APPLICATION: softly sculpted cheeks, jaw and temples to create a more oval shape. Applied midtone and contour color to the hooded area of the lid to help them recede and "open up" the eye. Subtle layering of color creates a very natural effect. Then a really well defined lashline makes the blue in her eyes stand out.

julie baker

SKIN LEVEL: 5 (medium)
FACE SHAPE: square-shaped face
EYE SHAPE: hooded eyes
SHADOWS: Highlight-shimmer beige
Midtone-matte taupe
Contour-matte mahogany

OBJECTIVE: to give the illusion of a more oval-shaped face. To minimize the hooded appearance of her eyelids, making her eyes to appear more open and alive.

APPLICATION: contoured the hairline and jaw to soften the " four corners". Highlighted down the center of the forehead, nose and the tip of the chin. Using midtone and contour colors, I applied, then blended them to the hooded area. This gave the illusion that the hooded area has receded.

jennifer hayler

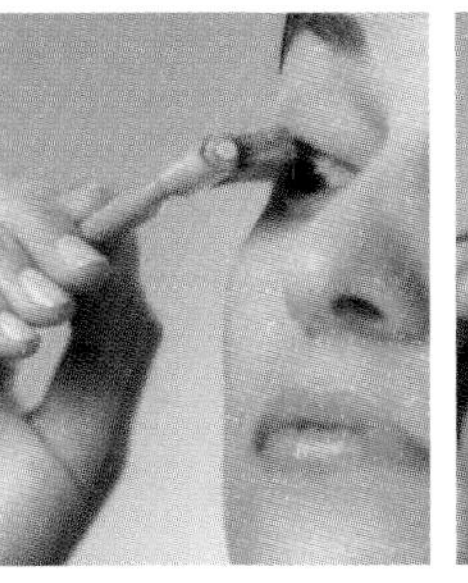
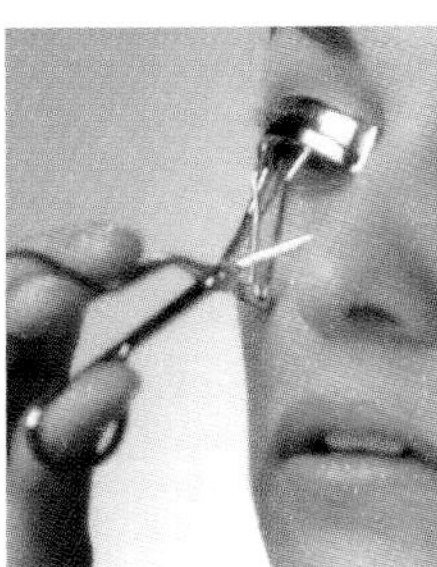
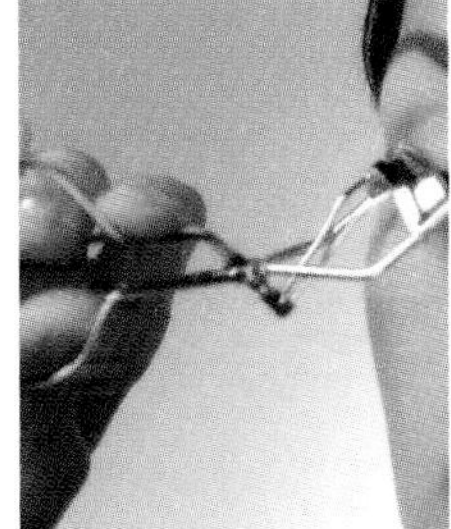
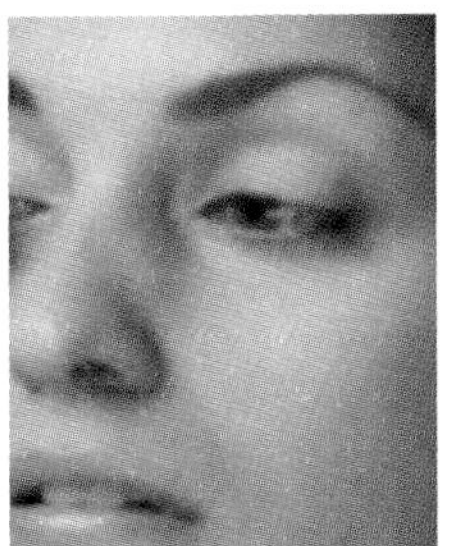
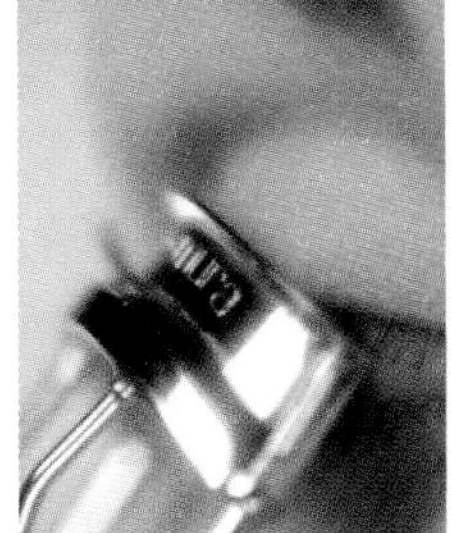
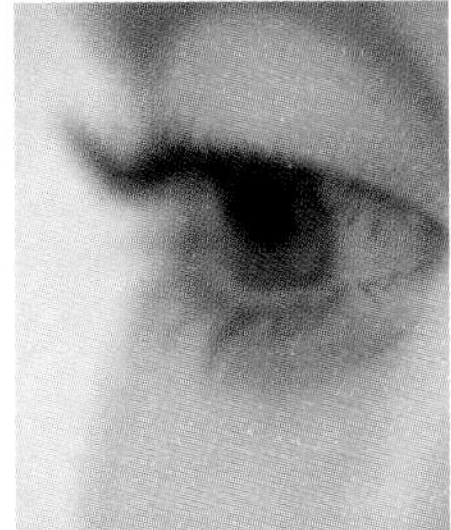

long lashes

Always curl your lashes because it opens up the eyes, making them appear larger and more youthful. Unfortunately it's a step many women skip, and it's a big mistake---so curl, curl, curl.

When curling lashes make sure not to just crimp them once. Instead, walk the eyelash curler up, starting at the base of your lashes, then crimp numerous times as you work the curler toward the tips of your lashes.

If you want your lashes to look thicker, work with your mascara-wand in a horizontal position. Start by applying your mascara at the root and work the wand in a side-to-side "sawing" motion, then sweep it out. In other words you're "scrubbing it" into your lashline then sweeping it along the length of the lash from root to tip.

If you want to lengthen your lashes, work with your mascara-wand in a vertical position. Begin at the roots and pull out to the tips.

Be sure you choose the correct mascara formulation for your desired effect.

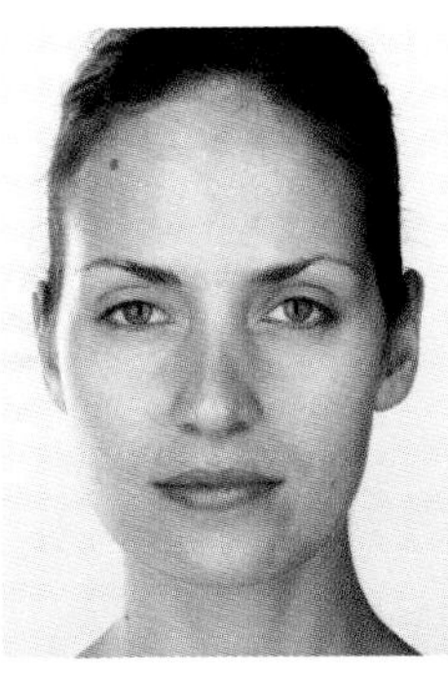

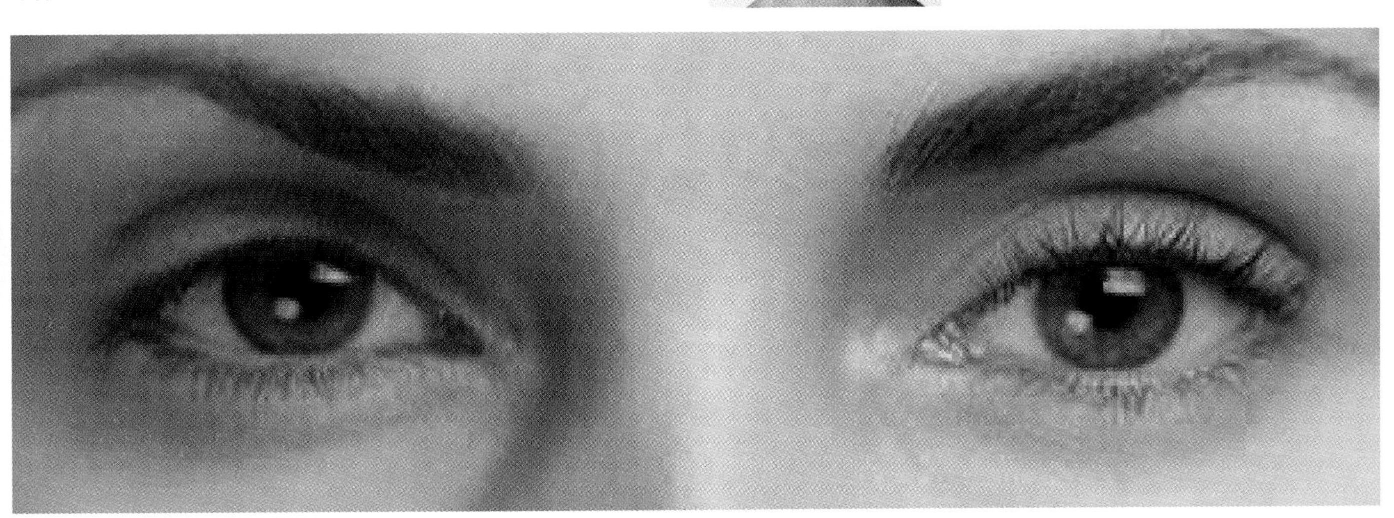

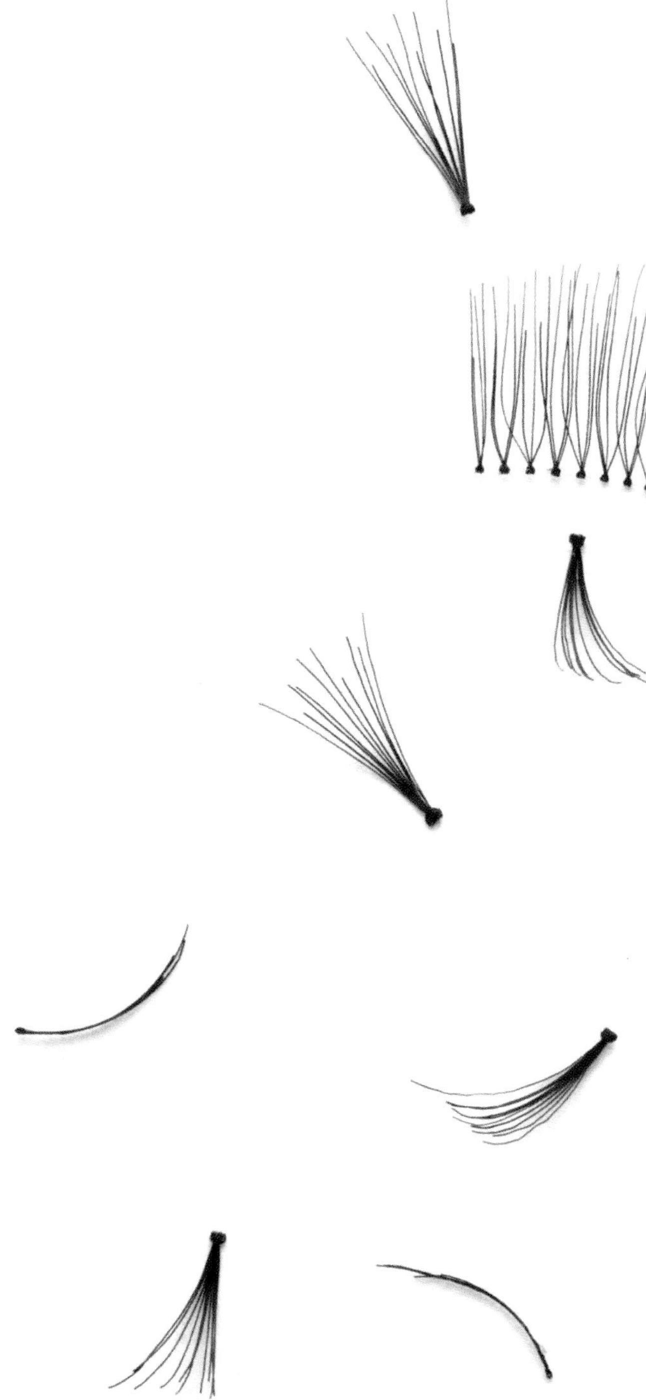

If you want more drama there are always false eyelashes. They come in STRIPS, INDIVIDUAL FLARE and INDIVIDUAL STRANDS.

If you'd like that flirtatious, "frankly fake" look for evening, use the strips because they are the most noticeable.

It's best to apply a pencil-eyeliner before your strip-eyelashes so you can see exactly where to place them and to prevent any skin from showing between your natural lashes and the false ones. The closer you place them to your natural lashline the more natural they'll appear. You can follow with a liquid liner to help disguise the lashes' band.

The flares are more natural-looking than strips, but my preference is for the individual-strand hair lashes. They look the most natural, and they are the ones usually used for most mascara advertisements. You simply apply them directly on top of your own lashes to help extend the length.

Tip: I personally prefer to use black mascara on the upper lashes but brown on the lower ones because brown looks less harsh.

Tip: Make certain you coat the lashes at the inside corners and the very outer corners. These are the ones many women miss.

Tip: Two or three thinly applied coats of mascara are far more effective than a single, "clumpy" one.

erica tracy

SKIN LEVEL: 4 (medium)
FACE SHAPE: square-shaped face

SHADOWS: Highlight-shimmer beige
Midtone-matte taupe
Contour-shimmer golden brown

OBJECTIVE: to give the illusion of a more oval-shaped face.
APPLICATION: contoured hairline and jaw to soften the "four corners" of the face. Highlighted down the center of the forehead, nose, and the tip of the chin. Made sure to highlight the lid and brow bone to open the eye. Defined the crease and lashline to give the eye more shape.

allison piro

SKIN LEVEL: 3 (fair)
FACE SHAPE: heart-shaped face

SHADOWS: Highlight-shimmer flesh
Midtone-matte taupe
Contour-shimmer golden brown

OBJECTIVE: to give the illusion of a more oval-shaped face.
APPLICATION: contoured her temples and the hollows of her cheeks to minimize the width. Highlighted the chin to create the illusion of more width. Made sure to define the lashline really well to intensify the color of the eyes.

SKIN LEVEL: 4 (medium)
FACE SHAPE: square-shaped face

SHADOWS: Highlight-shimmer beige
Midtone-matte taupe
Contour-shimmer golden brown

OBJECTIVE: to create the illusion of a more oval-shaped face.
APPLICATION: contoured the hairline and jaw to soften the " four corners" of the face. Highlighted down the center of the forehead, nose and the tip of the chin to create an oval illusion. Joanna has very unusually shaped eyes, to accentuate them I really highlighted and contoured them. Started by highlighting the lid and brow, then built contour in the crease and at the lashline.

brooke tobolka

SKIN LEVEL: 5 (medium)
FACE SHAPE: square-shaped face

SHADOWS: Highlight-shimmer beige
Midtone-matte taupe
Contour-shimmer dark brown

OBJECTIVE: to create the illusion of a more oval-shaped face.
APPLICATION: contoured the hairline and jaw to soften the" four corners" of the face. Highlighted down the center of the forehead, nose and the tip of the chin. Brooke has slightly hooded lids so using midtone and contour colors, I applied, then blended them to this area to help them recede. Then I made sure to define the lashline really well.

othercheeks

For me, applying cheek color is a two-step process because before I apply the actual cheek color, I bronze. I feel that just about everyone can benefit from bronzing because it warms up the face.

> Tip: Keep a separate brush for bronzers and blush because it keeps each color clearer and purer.

BRONZERS

Bronzers come in crèmes or powders and lend a healthy sun-kissed look without subjecting the skin to damaging ultraviolet rays.

To warm your face and accentuate your bone structure, simply dust bronzing powder across the contours and on the cheekbone. It's also useful for lightly sculpting the nose and chin.

Sweeping the bronzing powder up and around the temples and the eye socket can really help pop eye color---especially if your eyes are blue or green.

If bronzing powders and crèmes tend to look too bold on you, try using a pressed powder instead. Pressed powder has a lower pigment level and it blends really nicely. If you have lighter skin, ebony-toned pressed powders work beautifully.

When applying your bronzer, begin at the back of the cheekbone closest to the ear. Sweep forward, then go back and brush in the opposite direction to blend it well.

If you are using a crème, simply dot the color along your cheekbone, then blend. Don't forget a little at the temples to help shape your face.

BLUSH

Follow your bronzing powder with a light pop of blush applied to the apple of the cheeks. Using the correct blush color is paramount because you want to achieve a natural glow rather than a painted look.

Right off the top of my head I can think of three major mistakes women make with blush.

1. Using too much of it in the fall and winter to try to compensate for lack of sun.
2. Choosing a color that is either too red or too purple. Remember, to help determine a good shade for yourself, try a short burst of energetic exercise then match your blush color to your cheeks' natural flush.
3. Applying too little of a shade because it's too strong, therefore it doesn't last.

The amount or intensity of color you are wearing on your eyes and lips can be a factor in the amount of blush you might need that day.

For example, if you are wearing a strong lip color you will need less blush. If you are wearing a paler, sheerer lip color, you might need more blush.

A powder blush is the easiest and most commonly used.

When applying powder-blush, use your brush to brush it on starting from the front of the apples, sweeping back toward your ears.

If you'd rather use a crème or a liquid blush, you can apply it with either a sponge or your fingers. If you apply a creme or liquid blush before you powder your foundation, it will blend easier. If you'd rather wear your blush without foundation, a crème or a liquid blush works better than powder because it contains moisture that helps it blend well with the natural moisture in your skin.

To apply a crème or liquid blush, first dot a little onto the apples of the cheeks, blending back toward the ears.

Generally with any blush you should remember the rule to match the textures---crème on crème, powder on powder. However, if you want to increase the staying power of your crème-blush, you can dust a layer of powder blush over it. Remember to apply the crème blush before powdering, then the powder blush after powdering. It is the two layers of color that helps the staying power and color intensity.

> Tips: If, when you've finished applying your blush you feel it is too color-intense, it can always be softened with a dusting of loose powder.

> Tip: Never use blush to contour the face.

ashley cantley

SKIN LEVEL: 4 (medium)
FACE SHAPE: pear-shaped face

SHADOWS: Highlight-shimmer beige
Midtone-matte taupe
Contour-shimmer dark brown

OBJECTIVE: to give the illusion of a more oval-shaped face. Draw more attention to the eyes.

APPLICATION: contoured the jawline and the hollows of the cheek to help minimize their width. Highlighted the center of the forehead to help create width. To help bring attention to the eyes, defined the lashline and the crease really well.

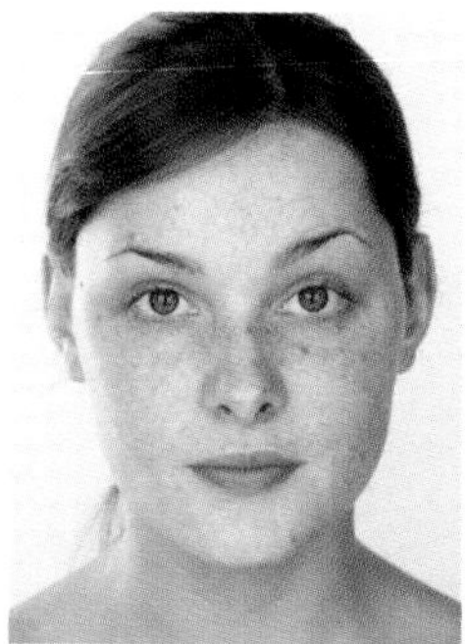

holly jonsson

SKIN LEVEL: 3 (fair)
FACE SHAPE: square-shaped face

SHADOWS: Highlight-shimmer flesh
Midtone-matte taupe
Contour-matte dark taupe

OBJECTIVE: to give the illusion of a more oval-shaped face. To define the features without the use of a lot of color.

APPLICATION: contoured the hairline and jaw to soften the "four corners". Highlighted down the center of the forehead, nose and the tip of the chin. I wanted a minimal look so I used much more subtle colors to define with, therefore giving you a practically no-makeup look.

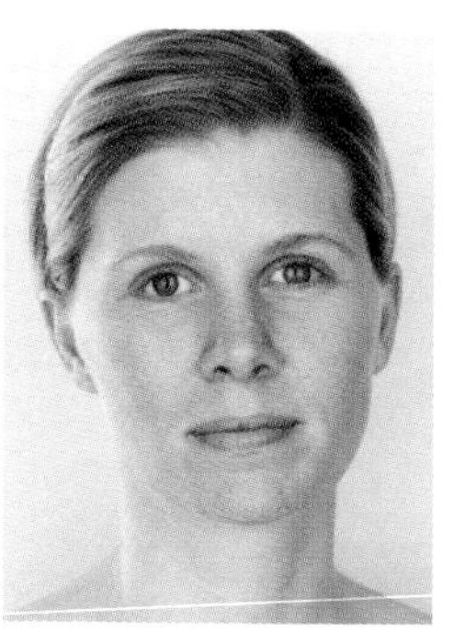

patricia young

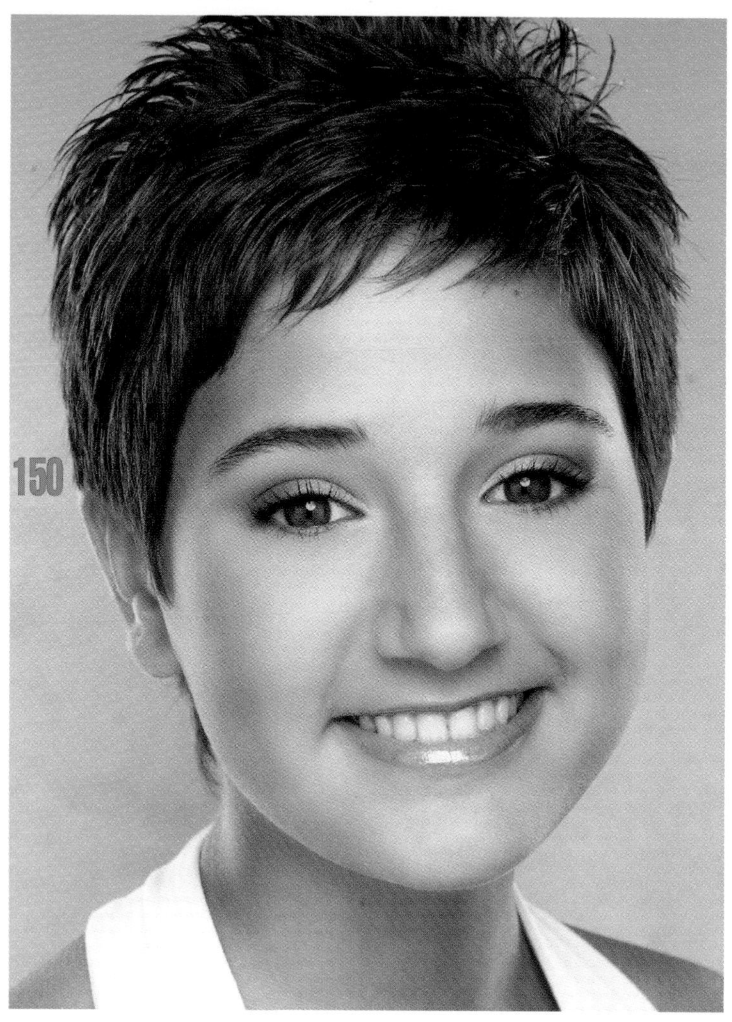

sidney helou

SKIN LEVEL: 8 (olive)
FACE SHAPE: square-shaped face

SHADOWS: Highlight-shimmer beige
Midtone-matte taupe
Contour-shimmer dark brown

OBJECTIVE: to give the illusion of a more oval-shaped face. To subtly define her features.

APPLICATION: her skin is so amazing that I certainly did not have to do much. Contoured hairline and jaw to soften the " four corners" of the face. Highlighted down the center of the forehead, nose and tip of the chin. Highlighted her lids and brow bones. Subtly defined her crease.

jordan helou

SKIN LEVEL: 6 (medium)
FACE SHAPE: square-shaped face

SHADOWS: Highlight-shimmer beige
Midtone-matte taupe
Contour-shimmer golden brown

OBJECTIVE: to give the illusion of a more oval-shaped face. To subtly define her features.

APPLICATION: contoured hairline and jaw to soften the " four corners " of the face. Highlighted down the center of the forehead, nose and tip of the chin. Highlighted lids and brow bones then defined eyes at lashline and in the crease. Finished with glossy lips.

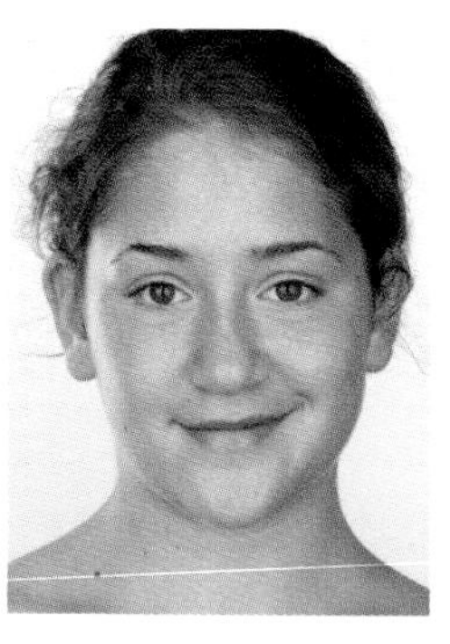

kathy helou

lips

90% of women have a fuller lower lip than top one, so don't feel bad if your lips are not perfectly even.

To keep lips looking luscious, exfoliate them once a week. I always prefer to use a little lip balm or moisturizer on the lips before I actually apply the lipstick because it evens the porosity and helps the lipliner and lipstick go on smoothly and more evenly.

Lip pencils will help prevent lipstick from feathering and bleeding, but once you've outlined your lips don't stop there. Be sure to blend inward so that when your lipstick wears off you aren't left with just an outline. You'll find a brush useful in the application and blending.

Make sure you optimize your entire mouth. Most women don't because they tend to draw inside the lip line. Conversely, take care not to overdraw because if you're using a lip color other than a natural lip-tone and you stray too far outside the lip line, it will be noticeable.

> Tip: Don't forget that brighter, warmer colors also make you look younger. Anything too dark is far too harsh for mature lips.

BASIC

To properly apply your lipliner to the top lip, begin with a V in the "cupid's bow" or center curve area of the lip. Then starting at the outer corners draw small, feathery strokes to meet the center V.

On the lower lip, first accentuate the lower curve of the lip, then begin small feather-like strokes from the outer corners moving towards the center.

Now you can actually apply your color.

You can use a brush, your fingers or a tube to apply your lipstick, but if it's applied with a brush it will usually look much more precise and last longer. For more intense color you can apply it straight from the tube, but it will be harder to cover the smaller detailed areas of the lips.

> Tip: Putting your lipstick on straight from the tube won't blend your lip-liner.

> Tip: Remember that paler colors illuminate and make lips appear fuller and more youthful while dark colors have a minimizing effect, making them appear smaller.

braden harris

vanessa shasteen

SKIN LEVEL: 4 (medium)
FACE SHAPE: pear-shaped face
SHADOWS: Highlight-shimmer flesh
Midtone-matte taupe
Contour-matte dark taupe

OBJECTIVE: to give the illusion of a more oval-shaped face. To subtly define her features without making her look to mature.

APPLICATION: contoured the jawline and cheeks to help minimize their width. Highlighted the center of the forehead to create the illusion of more width. Subtly defined the eyes at the lashline and glossed the lips to give her a fresh young look.

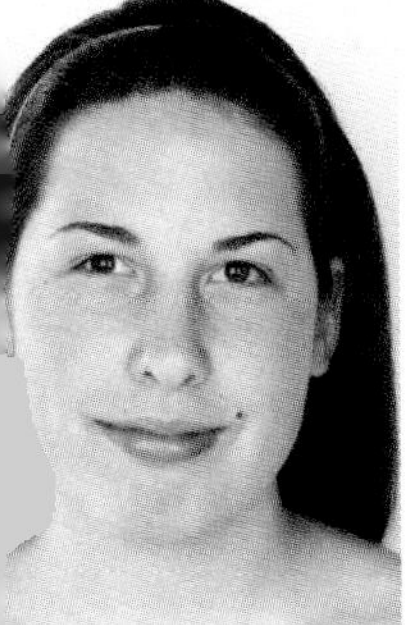

155

tess mullen

SKIN LEVEL: 4 (medium)
FACE SHAPE: oval-shaped face
SHADOWS: Highlight-shimmer beige
Midtone-matte taupe
Contour-matte dark taupe

OBJECTIVE: to softly define the features and give her a polished sophisticated look.

APPLICATION: with an oval shaped face there was not a lot for me to do. Wanted to warm up the skin, so applied bronze. Next, subtly defined the eyes by highlighting the lids and brow bone. Then softly defined the crease and lashline with soft colors.

stefanie cox

SKIN LEVEL: 6 (olive)
FACE SHAPE: square-shaped face
EYE SHAPE: wide-set eyes
SHADOWS: Highlight-shimmer beige
Midtone-matte taupe
Contour-shimmer dark brown

OBJECTIVE: to give the illusion of a more oval-shaped face. To help it appear as if the eyes are closer together.

APPLICATION: contoured the hairline and jaw to soften the " four corners" of the face. Highlighted down the center of the forehead, nose and the tip of the chin. Layered midtone color in the crease and on the inside hollow of the eyes to visually pull the eye placement closer together.

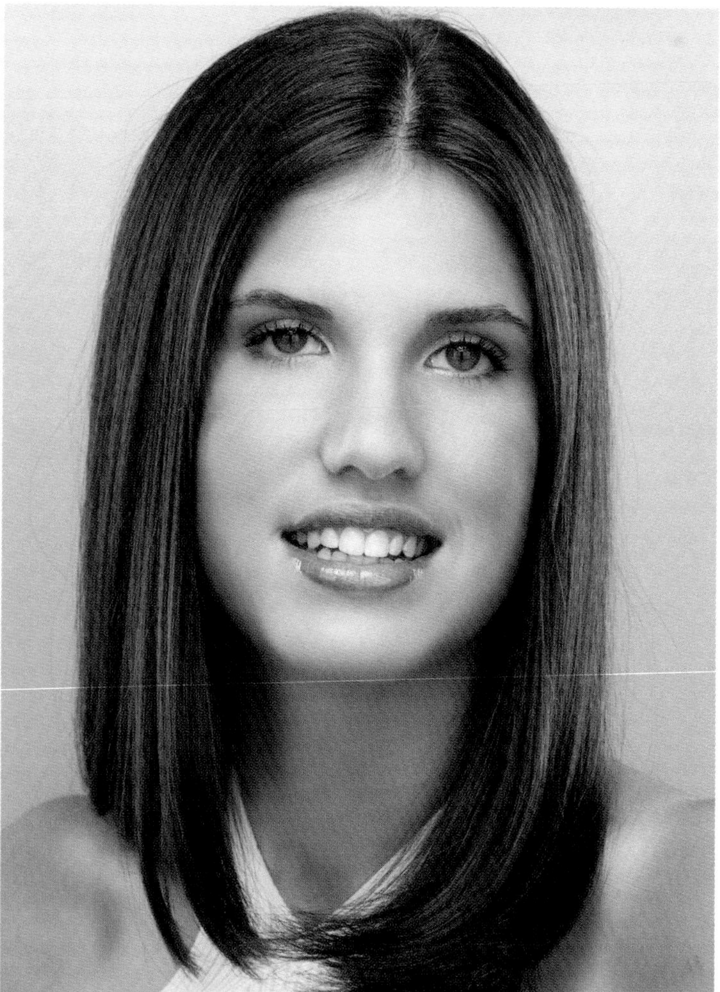

sarah bird

SKIN LEVEL: 5 (medium)
FACE SHAPE: pear-shaped face

SHADOWS: Highlight-shimmer beige
Midtone-matte taupe
Contour-matte dark taupe

OBJECTIVE: to give the illusion of a more oval-shaped face. To subtly define her features without making her look too mature.

APPLICATION: contoured the jawline and cheeks to help minimize their width. Highlighted the forehead to create the illusion of more width. Next, subtly defined her eyes at the lashline and highlighted her lids and brow bones.

amy williams

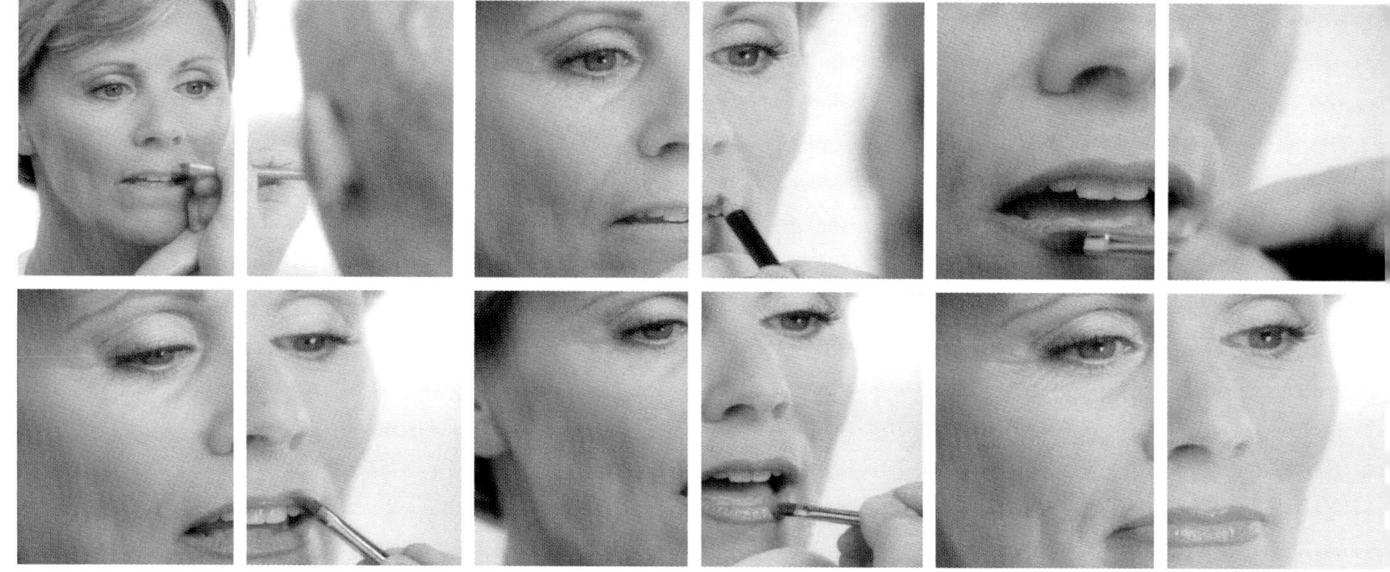

SMALL LIPS

If you feel you have small lips, the first thing you should do is erase your existing lip line with concealer. Doing this creates a fresh canvas on which you can design a whole new and improved lip line.

Using a natural-toned lipliner that is either the same shade as your natural lip color or one shade darker, draw your new lip shape on your top lip just outside your natural lipline. Follow the same procedure with your bottom lip. Then use the pencil to fill in, to help anchor the new lip shape.

You will now need two shades of lip color: a natural medium tone and a lighter shade, preferably glossy or shiny.

First, apply the darker shade to the outer edges of the lip, blending in the lipliner. Then apply your lighter color to the center of the mouth, making sure to blend the two shades together.This draws attention to the center of the mouth, creating the illusion of fuller lips.

Choosing the correct formula for the desired effect is paramount. Glossy is always sexy. Its shine makes the lips appear fuller and therefore more youthful. If your lips tend to be dry, stay away from matte lipstick. It's longer wearing but it will make your lips look and feel even more dehydrated.

Since crème formulas tend to work in just about any situation, they are always a safe choice.

Play with color. Don't be afraid of it. If it's wrong you can just wipe it off.

One last important point to remember. Never expect lipstick to last all day. Formulas that do just make the lips look parched and dry. These products contain stains that, unless your lips are freshly exfoliated, will adhere unevenly to the dry areas of your lips, causing your lipstick to appear splotchy and dehydrated.

Tips: Always moisturize your lips before applying color.

Tips: To help lipstick stay on longer, use lipliner all over your lips, apply lipstick on top, then blot and reapply.

Tips: To set your lipstick, try placing a single-ply tissue across your lips then lightly dust over it with a little loose powder.

debi moore

11 summary

Throughout the years I have been surrounded by beautiful, strong women, all of whom have greatly influenced my ideals of beauty.

My training in beauty began with many years of studying art, which I think is why I pay particular attention to the importance of shading, undertones and blending. My maternal grandfather was a talented artist and painter, so when my mother noticed very early on that I exhibited a similar gift I was encouraged to begin studying. As early as the sixth grade I won a scholarship to study painting and sculpture at the Museum of Fine Arts in Houston, Texas.

After many years of studying painting I grew tired of it, so I decided to focus my energy on acting. I then attended a high school for the performing arts and majored in theatre. That's where my interest in makeup really began, because along with performing in the productions I was encouraged to do the makeup for them. Actually it is there that I received my strongest encouragement to pursue my God-given talents in beauty. I then continued my education by studying all aspects of beauty, including hair and skin.

For as long as I can remember I have always been mesmerized by glamour. Like a lot of people of my generation, from a very early age I considered "Barbie" to be the absolute epitome of beauty and glamour. I have three sisters, and growing up we spent hours playing "Barbie". As far as we were concerned she had it all---beauty and brains.

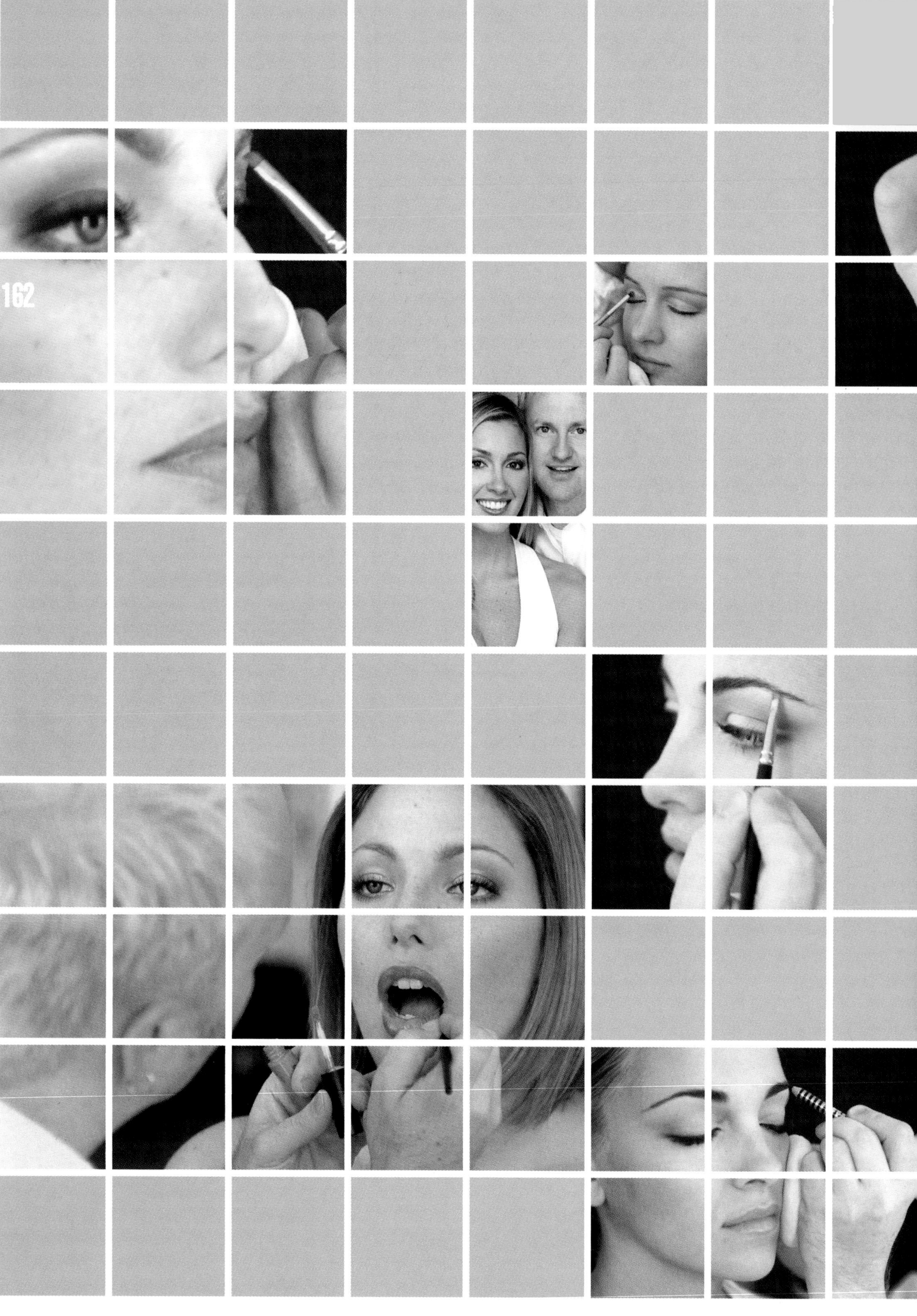

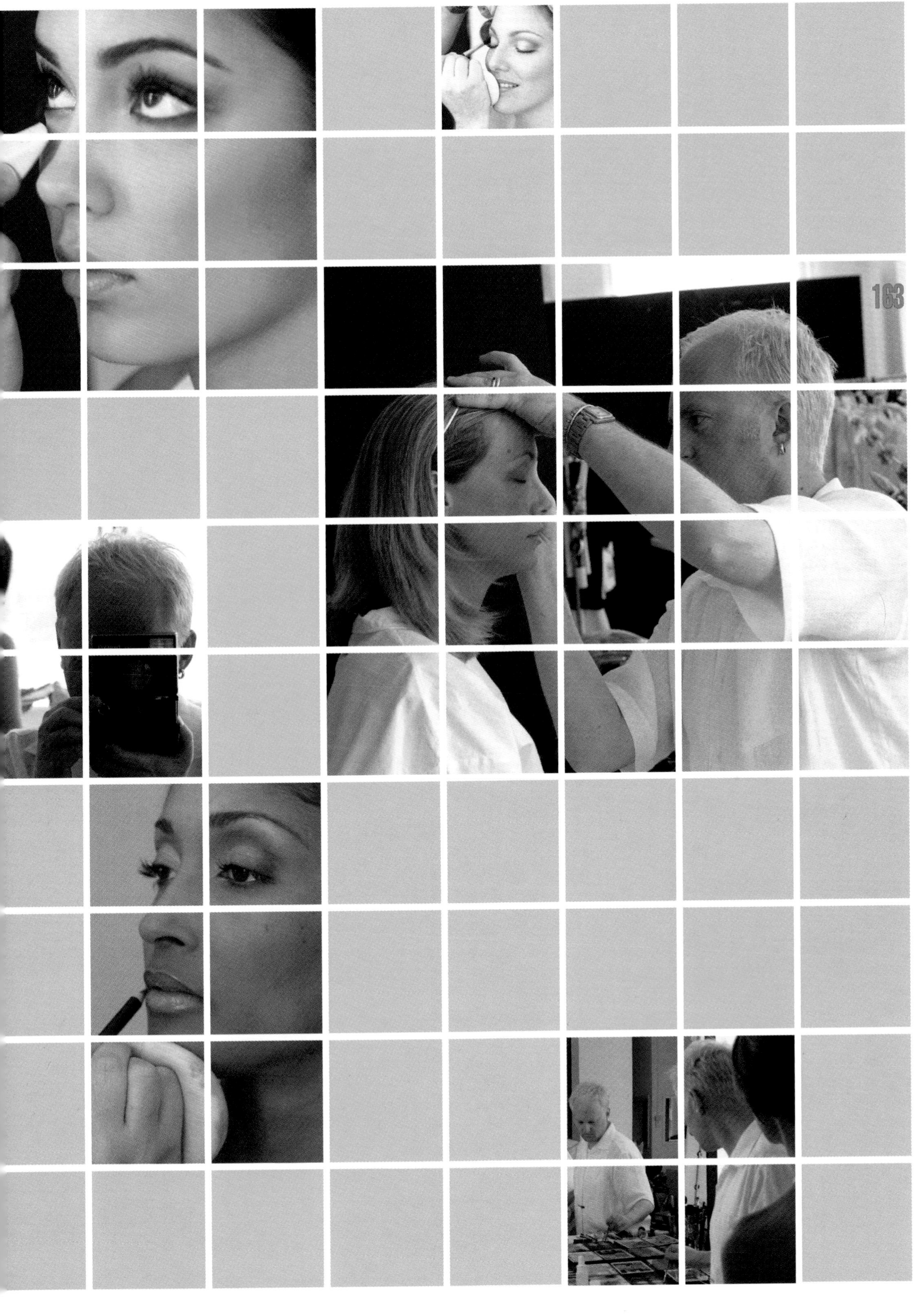

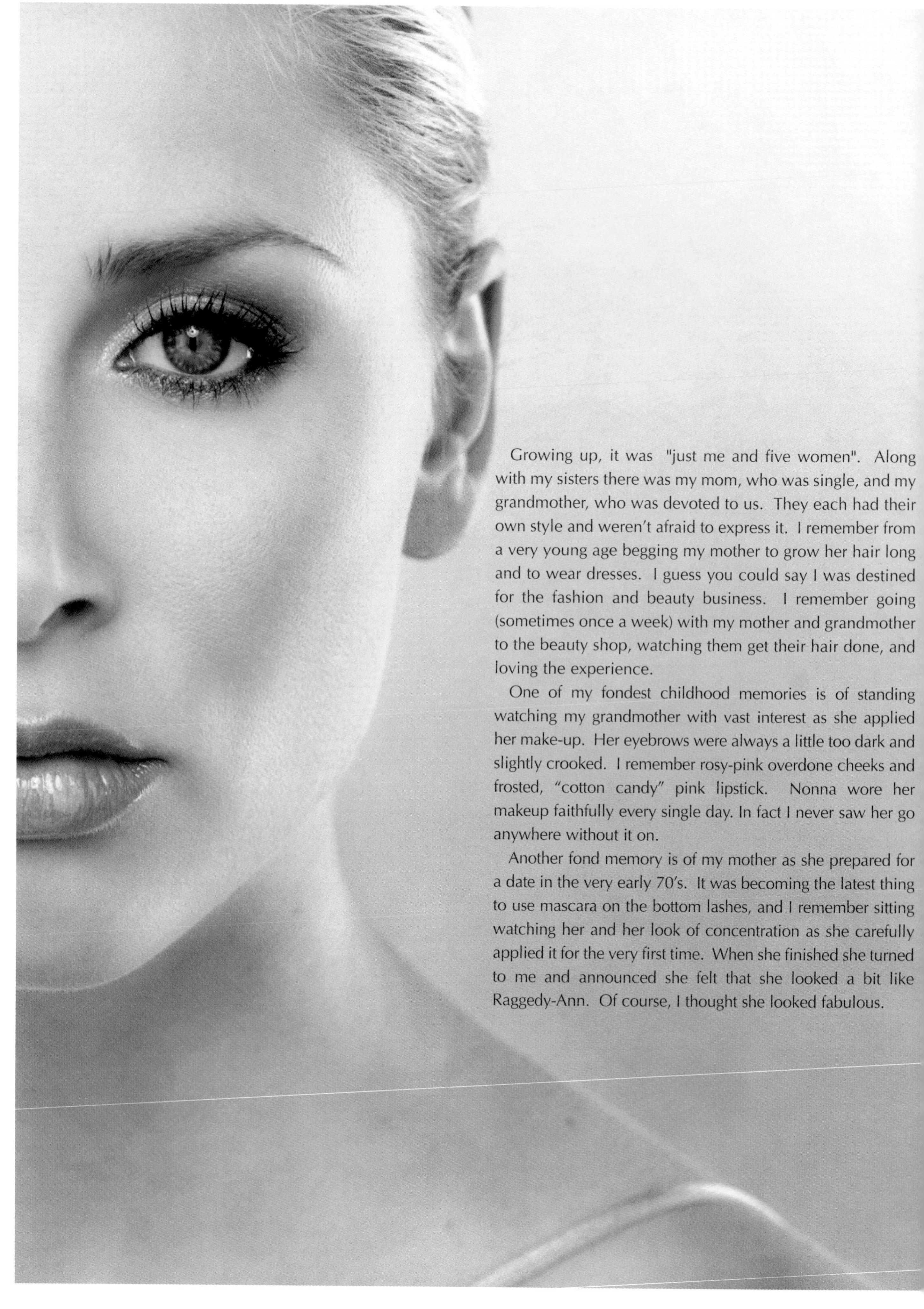

Growing up, it was "just me and five women". Along with my sisters there was my mom, who was single, and my grandmother, who was devoted to us. They each had their own style and weren't afraid to express it. I remember from a very young age begging my mother to grow her hair long and to wear dresses. I guess you could say I was destined for the fashion and beauty business. I remember going (sometimes once a week) with my mother and grandmother to the beauty shop, watching them get their hair done, and loving the experience.

One of my fondest childhood memories is of standing watching my grandmother with vast interest as she applied her make-up. Her eyebrows were always a little too dark and slightly crooked. I remember rosy-pink overdone cheeks and frosted, "cotton candy" pink lipstick. Nonna wore her makeup faithfully every single day. In fact I never saw her go anywhere without it on.

Another fond memory is of my mother as she prepared for a date in the very early 70's. It was becoming the latest thing to use mascara on the bottom lashes, and I remember sitting watching her and her look of concentration as she carefully applied it for the very first time. When she finished she turned to me and announced she felt that she looked a bit like Raggedy-Ann. Of course, I thought she looked fabulous.

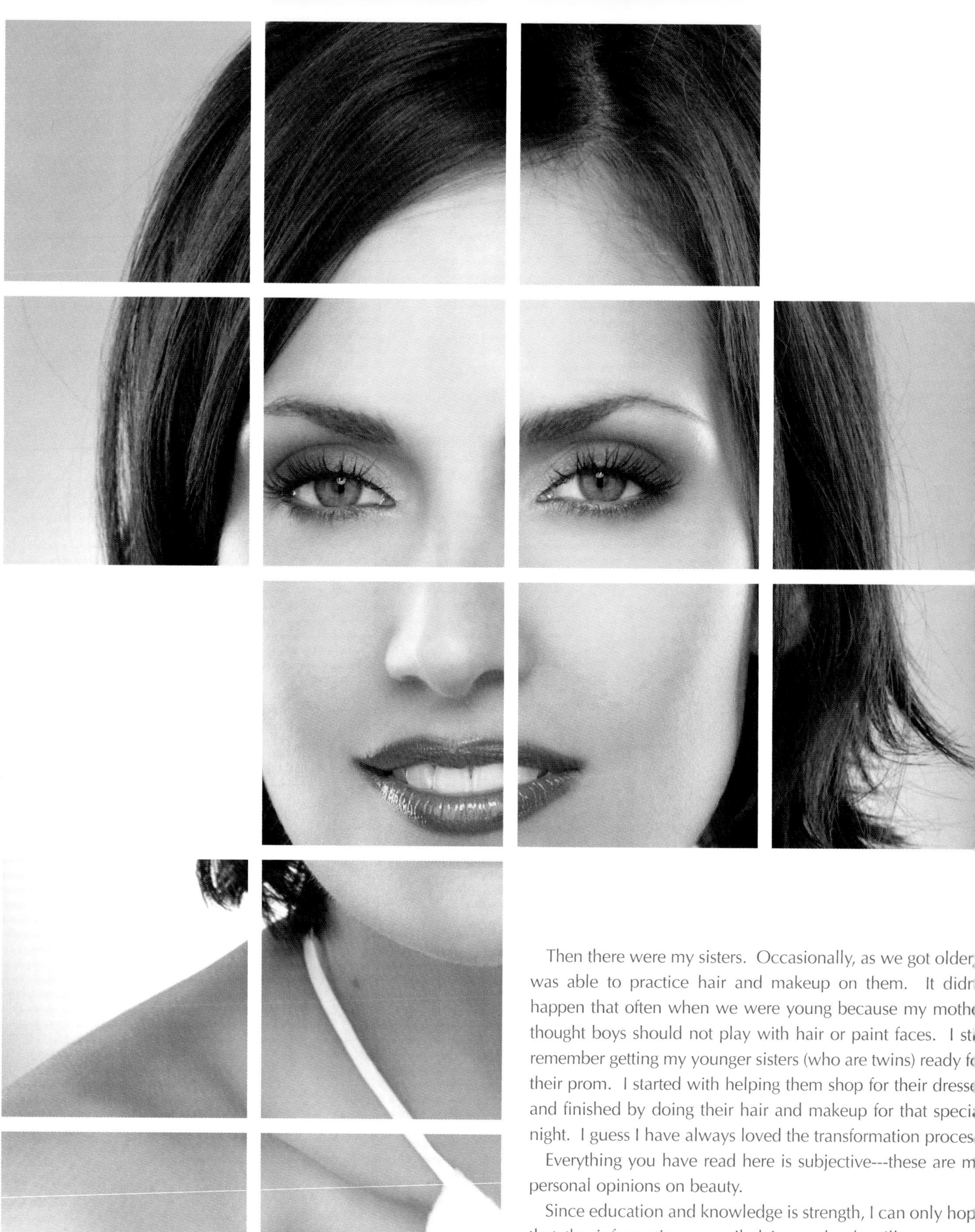

Then there were my sisters. Occasionally, as we got older, was able to practice hair and makeup on them. It didr happen that often when we were young because my moth thought boys should not play with hair or paint faces. I st remember getting my younger sisters (who are twins) ready f their prom. I started with helping them shop for their dress and finished by doing their hair and makeup for that speci night. I guess I have always loved the transformation proces

Everything you have read here is subjective---these are m personal opinions on beauty.

Since education and knowledge is strength, I can only hop that the information compiled in my book will encourag you, boost your self-confidence and help you to reveal you true beauty.

I can't impress upon you enough that it is so important to embrace your own personal beauty. Remember to love who you are, and enjoy where you are in your life today and everyday, because each and everyday will always be the first day of the rest of your life.

self confidence is the most important element of true beauty.

–robert jones

beauténotes